Teaching Students to Think Critically

A Guide for Faculty in All Disciplines

Chet Meyers

Teaching Students to Think Critically

Jossey-Bass Publishers
San Francisco • London • 1988

TEACHING STUDENTS TO THINK CRITICALLY
A Guide for Faculty in All Disciplines
by Chet Meyers

Library of Congress Cataloging-in-Publication Data

Meyers, Chet (date)
Teaching students to think critically.

(The Jossey-Bass higher education series)
Bibliography: p. 121.
Includes index.
1. Thought and thinking. 2. Reasoning. 3. Thought and thinking—Study and teaching. I. Title. II. Series.
LB1590.3.M49 1986 370.15′2 86-45627
ISBN 1-55542-011-7 (alk. paper)

Manufactured in the United States of America

The paper in this book meets the guidelines for permanence and durability of the Committee on Production Guidelines for Book Longevity of the Council on Library Resources.

JACKET DESIGN BY WILLI BAUM

FIRST EDITION
First printing: October 1986
Second printing: December 1986
Third printing: May 1987
Fourth printing: June 1988

Code 8627

The Jossey-Bass
Higher Education Series

Consulting Editor
Teaching and Learning

KENNETH E. EBLE
University of Utah

Contents

Part Three: Building Commitment to Critical Thinking in College

Preface

In recent years, educators nationwide have expressed concern over the inadequacy of students' ability to think critically. The development of thinking skills has always been a problematical aspect of teaching; but it is particularly acute today, when our culture's output of information far exceeds our ability to think critically about that information. Despite a growing body of literature on the subject, college teachers have found few suggestions for ways to improve the critical thinking of their students. Most of this literature has been highly theoretical, far removed from the practical concerns that constantly confront teachers and their students.

This book aims to help in bridging the gap between theory and practice in the teaching of critical thinking. It is written by a college teacher and addresses practical teaching concerns. It offers specific models for student assignments and exercises and also suggests a framework that can help teachers clarify their own understanding of critical thinking.

Most books about the teaching of critical thinking focus on the discipline of logic or on development of general problem-solving skills. This book departs from that tradition by suggesting that methods of critical thinking vary from discipline to discipline: Physicists go about this task differently than do historians or economists. Critical thinking should thus be developed in different ways by teachers in different disciplines. A corollary of this view is that teachers in *all* disciplines need to teach critical thinking *explicitly*.

This book also departs from traditional writing on critical thinking by emphasizing the importance of personal and subjective elements. Without denigrating the logical, objective approach that is traditional in the sciences and emulated by many other disciplines, the book suggests that personal interests, passions, and commitments, as well as esthetic elements such as beauty, mystery, and wonder, play a crucial role in developing attitudes that are necessary for critical thinking.

Finally, this book emphasizes that students must actively practice critical thinking by progressing through a series of increasingly difficult thought processes. Before students can develop a framework for critical thinking in any discipline, they must master the discipline's basic terms, concepts, and methodologies. Only then can serious probing, questioning, and analysis begin. Critical thinking skills develop best in an atmosphere of dialogue, interchange, and problem solving. Students do not learn much about critical thinking merely by listening to professors lecture.

Overview of the Contents

This book is divided into three sections. The first section provides basic concepts related to the teaching of critical thinking. Chapter One argues that logic and problem solving have serious limitations as vehicles for teaching critical thinking. It also presents a case for viewing critical thinking in the context of specific disciplinary perspectives. Chapter Two provides a framework to help teachers understand how the process of critical thinking may be taught. This framework draws on cognitive science and developmental theory, especially the work of Jean Piaget.

The second section of the book focuses on practical considerations of classroom teaching. It opens (Chapter Three) with a look at two programs that have been successful in teaching the attitudes and skills of critical thinking to college students. Chapter Four proposes that a sense of mystery and the desire to ponder and explore are essential parts of the motivation needed to develop critical thinking skills. It offers suggestions for creating a classroom environment that encourages these attitudes. Chapter Five helps teachers develop an interactive classroom environment in which discussion and problem solving replace lecture as a primary teaching strategy. Chapter Six offers models of written assignments—including summaries, short analytical papers, problem-solving exercises, outside assignments, and simulations—that teachers can use to help students practice critical thinking. Chapter Seven describes the advantages of a personal style of teaching, in which teachers discard an "objective," detached attitude and substitute active participation with students in the difficult task of sorting out subjective and objective elements in critical thinking. This chapter also briefly considers William Perry's insights on the ways subjective elements in students' thinking can interfere with the development of their critical thinking abilities.

Part Three focuses on the larger context for teaching critical thinking, first considering teacher preparation and then the social milieu in which such teaching takes place. Chapter Eight presents a model for critical thinking seminars, in which teachers from a variety of disciplines work together to design teaching strategies and student assignments, as an effective way to have "teachers teach teachers" about critical thinking. Chapter Nine concludes the book by presenting a brief summary of issues and considering the relationship between the teaching of critical thinking and larger cultural values.

While this book is designed primarily for teachers of undergraduate college students, it should assist any educator who is interested in practical approaches to the teaching of critical thinking. High school teachers and instructors of graduate students alike should find its framework helpful in developing ways to improve their students' thinking abilities. The chapter on teaching seminars should be of particular interest to administrators, who often must search for ways to stimulate and support their faculties in the struggle to improve teaching abilities.

I hope that this book's mix of models and methods will encourage more dialogue among teachers about the teaching of critical thinking. The best teachers often know implicitly how to present critical thinking skills. By working together and sharing their mutual concerns and wisdom, teachers can do much to improve their students' thinking abilities.

Acknowledgments

This book owes much to the unique collegiality that exists at Metropolitan State University. Without the support and contributions of the faculty and staff the book never would have come about. My thanks to the individuals who read drafts, created visual models and critical thinking assignments, and provided structure and support for my work on the book: Lois Anderson, Marjorie Corner, James Deegan, Leah Harvey, Melvin Henderson, Robert Gremore, Carol Lacey, Richard Niemiec, Susan Rydell, and Fancher Wolfe. I am indebted to Garry Hays, former chancellor of the Minnesota State University System, and to the staff at the Bush Foundation, who made my fellowship on critical thinking possible.

A special note of thanks to Kenneth E. Eble, who shepherded me through revisions of the text by providing the kind of tough editing every writer needs. Finally, my deepest gratitude to four colleagues: Catherine Warrick, who read and critiqued the overall text; Carol Holmberg, whose encouragement was unfailing and whose work on visualization was so key to the book's purpose; Tom Jones, who read text, provided assignments, and, as my officemate, put up with my harangues about the pains of writing; and to Miriam Meyers, wife, colleague, and friend, who contributed assignments, did all the initial editing, and provided immeasurable and invaluable support.

Minneapolis, Minnesota Chet Meyers
August 1986

The Author

Chet Meyers is professor of humanities at Metropolitan State University in Minneapolis. He received his B.A. degree (1964) from Allegheny College in sociology and his M. Div. degree (1968) from Yale Divinity School. Meyers served as coordinator of faculty training and development at Metropolitan State University for eight years and pioneered in the establishment of ongoing teaching seminars as a model for faculty development.

While Meyers's formal academic training is in the humanities, his informal training and interests are wide ranging. He has taught courses in adult education, human services, philosophy, and freshwater fishing. He has received recognition for his teaching excellence at his home university and in 1981 was awarded a Bush Fellowship to study approaches to teaching critical thinking. In addition to his university work, Meyers is an avid angler who writes articles and books on freshwater fishing.

Teaching Students to Think Critically

A Guide for Faculty in All Disciplines

1

What Critical Thinking Means Across the Disciplines

Concern with the development of critical thinking abilities in educational circles is not new. Its roots can be traced to Plato's Academy, the model from which modern Western universities ultimately arose. Colleges and universities came to depart from that earliest tradition and to focus more on the transmission of information, largely because of advances in the sciences and concurrent changes in educational goals. Today, however, the amount of information available through computers and the media seems to have outstripped people's abilities to process and use that information. In such a context, colleges and universities need no longer serve as repositories of knowledge, and teachers are no longer essential as lecturers and information givers. It is also increasingly important that students master the thinking and reasoning skills they will need to process and use the wealth of information that is readily at hand.

Educators' Changing Role

Malcolm Knowles suggests that, as a result of accelerating social change, educators must rethink their roles and concentrate on teaching students the skills and attitudes needed for self-directed inquiry. Reflecting on recent discoveries in the physical sciences and changes in approaches to other academic disciplines, Knowles states, "Facts learned in youth have become insufficient and in many instances actually untrue; skills learned in youth have become outmoded by new technologies" (1980, p. 28). In an age where textbooks are often outdated before they are off the press and most occupations experience rapid and perpetual innovation, the goals and aims of education inevitably must change.

Some educators foresaw the desired direction of this change long ago. In 1929 Alfred North Whitehead observed, "Your learning is useless to you till you have lost your texts, burnt your lecture notes, and forgotten the minutiae you have learnt by heart for the examination" ([1929] 1967, p. 26). His comment suggests that the real fruits of education are the thought processes that result from the study of a discipline, not the information accumulated. Even so, many colleges and universities continue to emphasize the learning of information and content rather than the development of thinking abilities. Thus, lecture remains a dominant mode of instruction. The lecture tradition fosters a generally passive style of education in which critical thinking is taught only implicitly or not at all.

Fortunately, this tradition of passivity is changing. The need to develop students' thinking abilities is being addressed in both a growing literature on critical thinking and recent innovations in curricula. Across the nation, colleges, secondary schools, and even primary schools are experimenting with a variety of methods for teaching students to think critically and analytically. In California, for example, the state college and university system now requires that every student complete a course in critical thinking before graduation (AFT News Release, July 12, 1985). Wisconsin's Alverno College has attracted national attention as a result of its curricular innovations, which teach students the skills of analysis and communication in a variety of disciplines (Loacker and others, 1984). And, even in the primary grades, Matthew Lipman's (1976) innovative program "Philosophy for Children" seeks to help young students develop the basic skills and attitudes needed for raising questions and thinking analytically.

Limitations of Logic and Problem-Solving Approaches

So how can we teach students to think critically? Most literature on the topic is highly theoretical, concentrating on attempts to define critical thinking. Good examples are Max

Black's classic work, *Critical Thinking* (1952), and Robert Ennis's article "A Concept of Critical Thinking" (1962). Definitions of critical thinking are usually made in terms of formal or informal logic or, in more recent years, of general problem-solving skills. Before we proceed with a more practical approach, it is useful to consider the limitations of these two popular theoretical viewpoints.

In Western culture, critical thinking traditionally has been closely identified with the discipline of logic. Logic formed an important part of classical models from which American education derives. In the early years of America's colleges and universities, logic often provided the philosophical framework for an entire curriculum. Aristotle's *Logic* and the principles of rhetoric were essential elements of the professional education of young gentlemen studying to become clergymen, teachers, doctors, or lawyers. Though the term *critical thinking* was not much in vogue in those days, the teaching of various forms of argument, syllogisms, propositional reasoning, and other logical operations was clearly seen as necessary to produce graduates with the keen thinking abilities appropriate to their chosen professions and standing in society.

Today, logic has become merely one specialized discipline among many. Nonetheless, many contemporary educators still view logic as the primary medium for learning the skills and attitudes of critical thinking. And students who have difficulty in demonstrating critical thinking abilities are often told to take courses in logic to remedy their deficiencies.

Other educators have sought to de-emphasize formal logic and, instead, develop critical thinking skills through courses in problem solving. (A typical text for such a course is *Creative and Critical Thinking,* by Moore, McCann, and McCann, 1985.) Such problem-solving courses may be taught under the auspices of departments of communication (reading and writing) or study skills centers. The courses often combine the teaching of basic logical operations (inferential reasoning, categorical propositions, syllogisms, and the like) with a process of problem solving derived from the methodology of the physical sciences. The process typically includes the steps of (1) recognizing and defining the problem, (2) gathering information, (3) forming tentative conclusions, (4) testing conclusions, and (5) evaluating and making decisions. Most general problem-solving courses attempt to communicate an objective, empirically based form of analysis with emphasis on the development of sound arguments and judgments. Students are taught to identify fallacies in reasoning, avoid contradiction, and recognize stated and unstated assumptions in the arguments of others.

Obviously, students can benefit from developing general problem-solving skills or studying logic. But both of these approaches have serious limitations as primary modes for the teaching of critical thinking. A major assumption underlying both approaches is that critical thinking skills are best taught in and of themselves, separated from specific subject matter. Once these skills are mastered, the theory goes, students can easily apply them to a variety of academic disciplines. The fact is that there is no simple equation between the skills of logic or general problem solving and the practice of critical thinking in specific disciplines.

Recent studies have suggested that there is little carryover between the understanding of the skills of logic and the application of good critical skills in other disciplines (Hudgins, 1978; McPeck, 1981). This is not surprising: Clearly, the rules of formal logic will have limited application to analysis of, say, a Picasso painting or a Virginia Woolf novel.

Teaching critical thinking through general problem solving also suffers a weakness inherent in all broad-based approaches to teaching. As John McPeck states, "The general skills approach to critical thinking represents a classical tradeoff. In its efforts to maximize the number of areas its general principles apply to, this approach must sacrifice genuine effectiveness in all of them. While its prescriptions are generally true, they are also hollow . . . for example: 'Make sure the conclusion follows,' 'Look out for tautologies,' 'Is a fallacy being committed?' 'Don't contradict yourself.' Such sage advice resembles a baseball manager exhorting his pitcher to 'throw strikes' " (1984, p. 39).

The identification of critical thinking with problem solving also assumes that critical thinking always begins with a problem and results in a solution. As we will discuss at length in Chapter Four, a central element in critical thinking is the ability to raise relevant questions and critique solutions without necessarily posing alternatives. Certain aesthetic elements of critical thinking—the pure pleasure of playing around with ideas—also clearly are not related to the instrumentality of problem solving.

Finally, one of the most serious difficulties with logic and problem solving as primary approaches to the teaching of critical thinking is that they encourage a sort of "academic buck passing." Teachers of composition commonly complain about students' poor writing abilities and attribute those deficiencies to poor teaching during the students' previous schooling. Similarly, if students can be channeled into courses in logic or problem solving, other teachers can relax because the difficult job of teaching students how to think will be done elsewhere.

On the contrary, teachers in all disciplines play a crucial role in the development of students' critical thinking abilities. Just as students will not become proficient writers merely by taking a year of composition but must be required to practice good writing in all their classes, so students will develop good critical thinking skills only by being challenged to practice critical and analytical thinking in the context of all the different subjects they study.

Discipline-Related Frameworks for Critical Thinking

In spite of their limitations, logic and problem solving do provide useful points of departure for more specific approaches to critical thinking. After all, critical thinking in all disciplines does incorporate basic elements of logical reasoning, especially those involved in making correct inferences or using deductive (if-then) reasoning to formulate sound judgments. Similarly, critical thinking in any discipline often takes the form of problem solving and/or analysis.

Nonetheless, both logical reasoning and problem solving take different forms in the context of different academic disciplines. As John McPeck suggests in *Critical Thinking and*

Education, "Thinking is always thinking about X, and that X can never be 'everything in general' but must always be something in particular" (1981, p. 4). McPeck wisely argues that critical thinking must necessarily vary among disciplines because the core ingredient of critical thinking is the foundational, or epistemic, knowledge of a given discipline. In other words, one cannot possibly think critically about history without a basic knowledge of the content and theory of history. That being true, history teachers clearly are much better equipped to teach critical thinking in history than are logicians.

In these circumstances, it should not surprise us to discover a variety of approaches to the teaching of critical thinking. Not only will critical thinking in literature differ in important respects from critical thinking in physics or history; no two literature professors will have the same definitions of critical thinking or teach critical thinking skills in exactly the same manner. For example, one literature teacher might teach students to analyze a novel by focusing on such things as character, plot development, symbolism, and uses of metaphor. Students could use these general concepts to develop a perspective for critically analyzing other novels. Another teacher might take a different but equally valid approach by presenting the novel as the product of a specific writer in a particular historical context. In this instructor's class, the teaching of critical thinking might focus on the way themes in a novel relate to an individual author's life and times, the ways an author's writing differs from that of earlier or later novelists, and the role of historical forces in shaping an author's definition of plot and character.

A similar variety of approaches will be found in other disciplines. Though teachers in the physical sciences are bound to a relatively uniform methodology, no two teachers of, say, geology will emphasize the same problems or issues.

No matter what specific approach is used, a teacher must present some explicit perspective or framework for disciplinary analysis—a structure for making sense of the materials, issues, and methodologies of the discipline being taught. To be sure, the identification of such a framework is not always easy. In organizing lectures and presenting information, teachers may rely on frameworks they know implicitly (their own critical thinking processes), but they may or may not be able to teach those frameworks to their students. Indeed, traditional college teaching all too often presents students with a welter of information and concepts and leaves them to struggle on their own to analyze, prioritize, and give structure to their newfound knowledge. Development of their critical thinking skills is thus haphazard.

I recall vividly from my own undergraduate education an example of how difficult learning a new mode of critical thinking can be. I had transferred from an engineering school, where I had gained a solid background in the methodology of the sciences and had also been introduced to logic and rhetoric. As part of the general education requirements of my new school, I had to take an arts course. I knew nothing about painting or sculpture, although, by the age of twenty, I was already imbued with a host of biases and preconceptions. Art seemed to me a totally subjective area of study, devoid of facts and sureties. There were no clear formulas to prove that something was or was not a work of art, and without a formula I, with my scientific background, was lost.

Had I been wiser, I would have pitied my instructor. His task bordered on the heroic. He not only had to pass on to me the cultural heritage of the arts but, in order to teach me to think critically about art, he had to restructure my whole perception of the discipline. For me a Picasso painting seemed nothing but a jumble, and my knowledge of logic was of little assistance in sorting things out. I had no understanding of form, perspective, color, or the traditions of the various schools of art. In short, I lacked a conceptual framework for making sense of art and thus had no organized basis for asking questions and forming judgments about works of art.

My instructor happened to be an excellent teacher, and he helped me develop a framework for critical thinking in art. After completing his course, I had learned a way of perceiving any work of art and formulating questions that helped me reach judgments about it. I learned to consider concepts such as the nature of subject matter, medium, form, perspective, and color and to appreciate the artist's intent and the influence of different schools of art on the artist.

The concepts I learned helped the engineering student in me create a formula for understanding art and thus formed the basis for the development of a new mode of critical thinking. This was the formula I arrived at:

> Subject + Medium + Use of key variables ⟶ considered in the context of a tradition + artist's intention = analysis

No doubt other students garnered something different. The point is that my instructor had done what teachers of critical thinking in any discipline must do, which is to provide—or give students the conceptual tools to develop—a basic framework for analysis of materials in that discipline.

General Attitudes Needed for Critical Thinking

A specific perspective or framework for analyzing materials and issues in a discipline is an important cognitive element in critical thinking. But affective elements can be equally important. These include general attitudes related to the raising of questions, temporary suspension of one's own judgments, and enjoyment of mysteries and complexities.

In his book *How We Think,* John Dewey defined the essence of critical thinking as "suspended judgment," or healthy skepticism ([1910] 1982, p. 74). He went on to spell out some qualities of "reflective thought" that might also be said to characterize critical thinking. "Active, persistent, and careful consideration of any belief or supposed form of knowledge in light of the grounds that support it . . . constitutes reflective thought" (p. 7). The staff of Alverno College recently echoed Dewey's insights. "Regardless of the discipline, we agreed, it was the nature of the college educational experience for students to question, examine, prod, poke, dissect, and explicate" (Loacker and others, 1984, p. 3).

Teaching a framework for analysis will be in vain unless students have the motivation to engage in critical thinking. To develop this motivation, students must actively struggle with real problems and issues—and see their instructors doing the same. If the instructor approaches critical thinking only in terms of some cut-and-dried objective methodology or merely rehearses students in the rediscovery of what is already known, students will acquire little motivation for critical analysis. Attitudinal aspects of critical thinking are better practiced than preached.

Luckily, teachers need not rely exclusively on their own resources to encourage student interest. Cognitive scientists argue that inquisitiveness and certain thinking abilities are innate features of the human species (Hunt, 1982b). Children possess a natural curiosity and desire to explore their physical and psychological environments, as any parent can attest. Most also accomplish one of life's most difficult cognitive tasks, the learning of language, with a wonderful innate ability. But sad to say, by the time students reach college, the inquisitiveness of many has been stifled. In classrooms and homes that discourage attitudes of inquiry and skepticism, children quickly learn to remain silent rather than risk embarrassment and disapproval by asking questions that teachers or other adults may consider dumb.

College instructors must strive to create a classroom atmosphere in which students' natural inquisitiveness can once again come to the fore. As John Holt, a longtime critic of traditional pedagogy, remarks, "We don't have to make human beings smart. They are born smart. All we have to do is to stop doing things that make them stupid" (1982, p. 161). In Chapter Four we will explore strategies for creating a classroom environment in which discovery, exploration, and questioning are encouraged and fostered.

The Active, Building-Block Nature of Critical Thinking

Once students' interest has been captured, it must be retained and built upon. To retain interest and develop students' critical thinking abilities to the fullest, the classroom environment must be highly interactive. Students cannot be mere sponges, absorbing the "wisdom" of a teacher's lecture. Rather, they must realistically engage subject matter and actively practice the art of critical thinking.

One might smile at the idea of a college course in basketball in which students spend all their time learning basketball terminology, diagramming plays, and watching videotapes of the Boston Celtics setting up plays. Then, for the final exam, students are expected to play a competent game of basketball and maintain a shooting average of 50 percent. Yet this is similar to what occurs when teachers spend the bulk of classroom time lecturing, presenting theory, and testing for recall of information and then expect students to demonstrate good critical skills in a final term paper or student project.

In traditional teaching there is often an implict assumption that learning to think critically develops *naturally* as students learn increasingly complex levels of discipline content and information. While there may be a natural basis for human inquisitiveness, there is nothing natural about learning a framework for analyzing a modern novel or management system. Analytical frameworks must be taught explicitly and constructed consciously, beginning with simple operations and building toward complexity and subtlety. Initially, for most students, this means learning to recognize key concepts, terms, issues, and methodologies—not by memorizing them but by working with them in the context of real problems and concerns and by relating them to experiences and previous learning.

Creating frameworks or perspectives for critical thinking takes time, patience, and the intentional design of classroom exercises and assignments that force students to practice critical thinking. In Chapters Five and Six, we will consider practical aspects that will help instructors create environments and exercises that will encourage the skills and attitudes of critical thinking.

2

Examining the Process of Critical Thought

What goes on in our brains when we solve a problem in physics or analyze a Hemingway novel? How do experts and novices differ in the ways they analyze issues and solve problems? What methods can teachers use to help students learn specific approaches to critical thinking that are appropriate for different disciplines? What can college teachers learn from cognitive scientists and developmental theorists that will help them teach critical thinking?

Morton Hunt summarizes recent developments in the rapidly changing field of cognitive science. He stresses the human brain's innate abilities. "Research suggests that our minds come equipped with highly efficient neural arrangements built into us by evolution; these predispose us to make certain kinds of sense of our experiences and to use them in that distinctly human activity we call thinking" (1982a, p. 13A). Hunt goes on to argue that humans are "concept-making creatures" and that we use our innate thinking abilities to categorize, generalize, and in other ways make sense of the world.

The equipment, ability, and general predisposition to think may be innate, but the specific ways in which we make sense of the world are learned. They are also poorly understood and very complex. Some scientists believe that the healthy human brain has the capacity to store as many as 100 trillion bits of information—more than 500 times the amount of information contained in an entire set of *Encyclopaedia Britannica* (Hunt, 1982b). Researchers are just beginning to understand how this vast capacity for storing information is used in thinking processes.

Studies comparing the problem-solving techniques of experts and novices offer some interesting observations. To study such techniques, scientists have presented individuals with a problem and then asked them to talk out loud as they thought the problem through, verbalizing their thoughts as quickly as possible. By analyzing what different people said, researchers discovered some important aspects of critical thinking.

Hunt (1982b, p. 140) cites a report by Paul Johnson, of the University of Minnesota, that shows how an expert cardiologist, when presented with only a few scraps of information, formulates a correct diagnosis. Such an expert can analyze problems quickly because he or she has a wealth of previous experience in working with the materials, issues, and problems of his particular discipline. The information from those previous experiences is structured and prioritized through practice so that it is readily available for analyzing problems and issues.

When novices in any field attack a problem, they develop a hypothesis and follow a lead until it results in a dead end. Then they backtrack and start over with another approach. Novices also typically have difficulty prioritizing issues and sorting out variables; they act as if all considerations have equal importance. The experts, on the other hand, quickly identify central variables, eliminate noncrucial considerations, and, drawing on their vast previous experience of related problems, formulate an analysis (Hunt, 1982b, p. 264). They are able to do this because they possess a framework for analysis, some structure for making sense of things and organizing experience. How such frameworks or structures develop is an important consideration in teaching critical thinking.

Mental Structures: The Contributions of Jean Piaget

The Swiss psychologist Jean Piaget has developed a number of helpful analogies for describing how the human brain seems to structure and make sense of experience. Piaget's work derives from years of closely observing and talking with young children as they worked and played, noting the ways they solved everyday problems. His insights about how children solve increasingly complex problems provide a helpful perspective for thinking about the teaching of critical thinking skills and attitudes.

Piaget (1976, p. 119) insists that children do not receive knowledge passively but rather discover and construct knowledge through activities. As children interact with their psychological and physical environments, they begin to form what Piaget calls structures for thought. These structures help to organize the children's experience and direct future interactions. Piaget envisions the structures as problem-solving methods or blueprints for guiding behavior. The infant's first structures are sensorimotor—for example, developing the hand-eye coordination necessary for thumb sucking or manipulating toys in the infant's crib. As the child grows, more complex mental structures are added.

As long as a particular structure works, it will guide a child's interactions. Sooner or later, however, the child's blueprints are bound to be challenged. As two of Piaget's followers note, "Owing to the child's inborn drive to interact with his environment, he meets contradictions, that is, things do not fit his present mental structures. These contradictions produce a state of disequilibrium. In other words, the child's present mental structures are found inadequate and must be altered or replaced" (Lawson and Renner, 1975, p. 337). As we grow older, we come to have a greater investment in maintaining our old blueprints for interaction, but we will still modify them (and when necessary create new ones) when circumstances create enough disequilibrium.

Although Piaget's work describes young children, we can draw on his concept of structures when discussing learning processes in college students. If we view mental structures as components of larger disciplinary perspectives for problem solving and analysis, we can say that when we teach students to think critically, we are helping them alter or replace their mental structures.

Piaget's description of equilibrium and disequilibrium is also useful in that it provides a perspective for understanding some of the tensions involved in teaching critical thinking. The process of modifying old, or creating new, mental structures is often uncomfortable and at times even painful. This is especially true when blueprint modification involves not merely the rearrangement of mental furniture but major structural renovations.

Such major renovations are most likely to occur when students explore new disciplines. If students have entered college with rather sparse mental accommodations, they may find themselves being asked to adopt completely new ways of perceiving the world. Exposure to a multiplicity of new ways of thinking in the early college years can be very disconcerting. Some degree of student discomfort, however, is inevitable and ultimately beneficial. Teachers should be acutely aware of the inherently disruptive nature of this educative process. Teaching critical thinking involves intentionally creating an atmosphere of disequilibrium, so that students can change, rework, or reconstruct their thinking processes.

One reason that reconstructing thinking processes can be painful is that structures of thought are not merely matters of dispassionate cognition. They are also highly personal and emotional, involving cherished values and beliefs. Personal beliefs and values serve as a perceptual grid through which experience is screened. As Yinger points out, "As a result of our experience, each of us has 'implicit theories' about the world and the way in which it functions. Implicit theories are the unexamined or unconscious theories that allow us to structure, interpret, and make sense of our world. . . . Together they constitute our belief system and our personal perspective. Implicit theories become the lens and filter for everyday experience, dictating what one sees and how one interprets it" (1980, p. 16). Part of teaching critical thinking necessarily involves challenging students' implicit theories and teaching them new perspectives for interpretation. It can thus become a very emotion-laden process.

I am reminded of a story a colleague tells about an adult student in one of her introductory linguistics courses. After the fifth week of class, this student approached her teacher and complained bitterly that she was not getting out of the course what she wanted. The student said, "Look, all I wanted to learn in this class was something about correct and incorrect English usage. But you're telling me that some forms of expression are proper today, while my English teacher twenty years ago taught me they were wrong. Who's right? What's proper and what isn't?"

An important part of the critical thinking process that my colleague was trying to teach her students had to do with the dynamic aspects of language and with raising questions about the nature of language. What was "standard English" in Shakespeare's day, or even twenty years ago, may no longer be standard. But this student was looking for the "right" answers to usage questions—the right answers for all time. My colleague's relativistic approach was challenging the student's mental structures and implicit theories, causing great conflict. The teacher was asking the student to be flexible and change the way she thought about language, and the student, stuck in her old ways of thinking, was experiencing the pain of disequilibrium.

Some students handle disequilibrium better than others, but all students have their limits. Teaching students new thinking processes involves gauging very sensitively the amount of disequilibrium that will do the most good. Too much can overload students and be dysfunctional, while too little can result in warm, wonderful classes where no learning takes place. A friend of mine suggests that the best teachers are those who know how to create and maintain a proper balance between challenge and support, and I agree wholeheartedly. One of the keys to teaching critical thinking successfully is to simultaneously challenge students' old modes of thinking and provide structure and support for the development of new ones. We will explore these personal aspects of critical thinking in more depth in Chapter Seven.

Making Implicit Thought Processes Explicit

When we see a juggler effortlessly tossing oranges in the air, we fail to appreciate the first stumbling efforts and the hours of practice that laid the groundwork for that proficiency. The same holds true for expert critical thinkers. All experts started as novices—struggling with basic concepts, questions, and issues—as they developed the thought processes that would help them make sense of things. The problem is that by the time they have achieved their expertise, many of those thought processes have become so automatic, internalized, and implicit that the experts have difficulty explaining explicitly how they think.

Teachers are experts, too. By the time most college teachers have completed their undergraduate and graduate education, they have spent thousands of hours immersed in the terminology, concepts, issues, and methodologies of their disciplines. The ways they critically analyze issues and problems have often become second nature to them. Although they may demonstrate their critical thinking abilities implicitly in the ways they organize lectures, raise questions, and engage students in discussion, they may have trouble providing the explicit formulations that students need in order to develop their own critical thinking abilities.

In the initial stages of teaching undergraduates to think critically, the wise teacher will avoid overwhelming them with the intricacies of the process. Instead, the instructor should focus on teaching the basic disciplinary foundations—terms, concepts, issues, methodologies, and so on—and providing general ways to structure that knowledge and begin asking questions about it. In other words, the teacher should create the foundation for a framework of analysis. This is not to suggest that teachers "spoon-feed" their students by oversimplifying, but simply that they take time to structure the information they present. When students see some order or sense in things, they are much more likely to be able to recall information and apply what they have learned.

One of the pioneers in the study of retention, F. C. Bartlett, demonstrated that an important function of memory is to reconstruct or structure information according to one's initial assumptions and beliefs about "what must have been true." Bartlett discovered that "people tended to interpret information in terms of previously acquired knowledge and concepts, which in turn influenced their recall of the material" (Bransford, 1979, p. 156).

The message of this finding for teachers of critical thinking is that if they do not offer a framework for making sense of the content of their courses, students will provide their own. And the framework that students provide for themselves may not help them develop the analytical skills that their teachers want them to learn. As Norman notes, "We found it essential to provide the prototype model for the students. . . . If you as a teacher do not provide the model, the student is likely to pick one anyway, and if you are to have any control in the situation, it is best for you to have made the selection" (1980, p. 44).

Visualizing the Critical Thinking Process

As we have noted, making one's implicit analytical framework explicit can be difficult. Many teachers, like other experts, have great trouble with this task. One way to make the job easier is through *visualization*. In this process one tries to envision, as best one can, what one's thinking processes "look like." I have learned from personal experience that this technique can be very rewarding.

Over the years I have been involved in numerous workshops on setting course objectives for critical thinking, and I have usually left them with a sense of frustration. For one thing, they are usually too theoretical. For another, the limited workshop format does not afford enough time for teachers to undertake the demanding process of clarifying critical thinking concepts. Finally, one-shot workshops do not provide the psychological support necessary for making significant changes in one's teaching methodology.

Attempting to remedy these deficiencies, I recently had the opportunity to design an ongoing seminar that would allow an extended period of time for faculty to clarify teaching goals related to critical thinking and would provide group support for implementing change. (This seminar is described more fully in Chapter Eight.) In the initial seminar, a group of eight faculty agreed to meet one evening a month for six months to work on clarifying the exact nature of their teaching objectives and to focus specifically on the thinking skills they wanted students to learn. The group also planned to share teaching strategies and written assignments designed to test critical thinking.

It was a big agenda for six meetings. What actually happened was that the group spent the entire six months helping one another "talk through" teaching goals and definitions of critical thinking. It became clear that each person in the seminar had a fair idea of what he or she wanted to teach in terms of *content,* but few had ever taken the time to spell out any organized framework for thinking *processes.* Although everyone found the seminar helpful, we fell short of our individual and group goals in identifying specific approaches to critical thinking.

Fortunately, in the same year that I initiated my teaching seminars, a colleague, Carol Holmberg, was struggling with what turned out to be a related problem. For years Holmberg had been trying to teach adult students to read literature critically and had encountered many of the same frustrations that teachers of normal-age undergraduates do. Despairing of lecture and discussion techniques, she decided to attempt a new approach. In a paper entitled, "Using Visual Paradigms in Classroom Teaching," she describes how the inspiration for this new approach occurred.

> One evening some years ago, while struggling to teach the essentials of a complex novel to a Twentieth Century Literature class, I asked myself, "What do you *really* want your students to master of this writer's work?" The answer came: "The principles of perception which guide the artist's aesthetic experience." To illustrate this point, I turned to the blackboard and drew a simple sketch, developed as a result of some earlier work on William Blake. I wished to illustrate that artistic products reflect "degrees of perception" . . . and that the process of perception usually begins with a concrete, or sense-focused, experience . . . and "expands" to encompass more comprehensive patterns of thought and feeling reflected in our social, philosophical, and cultural traditions. . . .
>
> What had actually occurred that evening so long ago? I was simply "translating" that elusive process called "thinking" into something that students could actually see (albeit metaphorically) and more easily grasp [1982, pp. 1–2].

Holmberg's sketch, depicted in Figure 1, is a visualization of one possible framework for critical thinking in literature. One

Figure 1. Visual Model of Modes of Perception in Literature.

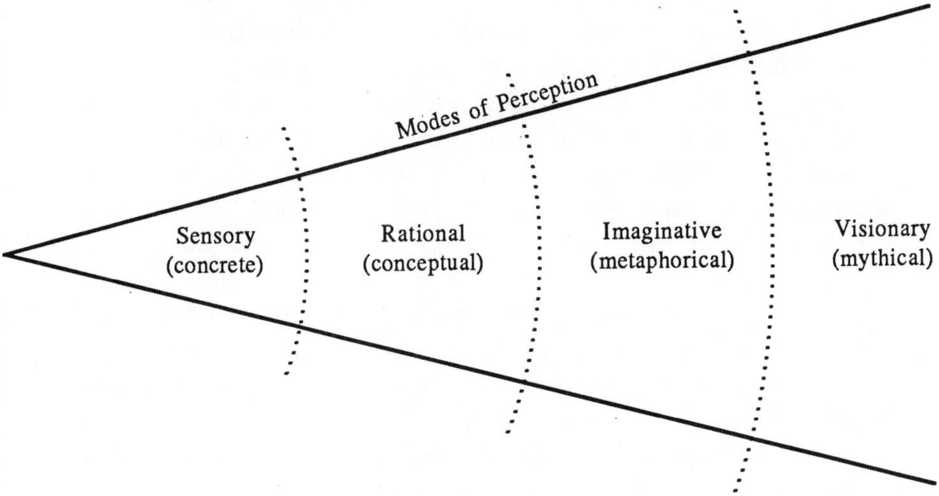

Source: Holmberg, 1982, p. 1. Used by permission.

of Holmberg's primary teaching goals was to move her literature students beyond narrow, literalistic perceptions of prose to more expanded interpretations that incorporate the richness of imaginative metaphor and visionary imagery. Her model illustrated one way to conceive of this movement. It became an organizing principle for her class and resulted in the development of increasingly critical modes of perception in her students.

In her four-stage model, Holmberg began where students' perceptions of literature usually start—at a concrete, sensory level. For example, *The Plague,* by Albert Camus, is, on a sensory level, a novel about a plague with ghastly implications for the people of Oran. The rats, pustular boils, and stench of death are all part of that sensory level. On a rational level, the book describes a disease with its own logic that must be combated by the rational resources of medicine, exemplified by Dr. Rieux. On a metaphorical level, Camus may be making a statement about the effect World War II had on separating individuals from things they love. Finally, on a visionary or mythic level, Camus may be using the idea of the plague to make a personal philosophical statement about the human condition.

Holmberg's work is important for the teaching of critical thinking because it uses a concrete, visual image to explain an abstract process of thought, thereby making that thinking process more accessible to students. Holmberg herself quickly realized this. Her model worked so well in her own classes that she began sharing her ideas with other teachers. She held a number of workshops in which she offered this visual model as a tool for teachers to use in moving their students to higher levels of analysis and critical thought. Whether or not they decided to use that particular model, almost all the people who attended Holmberg's workshops found the attempt to visualize the ways they analyze disciplinary materials worthwhile.

After attending one of Holmberg's workshops and seeing how eagerly teachers participated in attempts to visualize their thinking processes, I saw a possible answer to the frustrations in my own critical thinking seminars. Our attempts to "talk through" teaching goals related to critical thinking had remained at a much too abstract, theoretical level. The use of a concrete visual image did more to make explicit the implicit concepts of critical thinking than any amount of talking could ever have accomplished.

When I began a second series of seminars the following year, I asked Holmberg to present her visual model at the first seminar meeting. She then asked those present to draw, as best they could, a visual representation of the critical thinking process they wanted their students to master by the end of their respective courses.

The results were dramatic. Though the artistic level of some participants extended little beyond drawing stick figures, some powerful visualizations emerged. After two additional seminar sessions in which participants helped each other clarify the design of their visual models, a number of teachers said that, for the first time in their careers, they were beginning to understand not only the critical thinking skills they wanted students to learn but their own overall teaching objectives as well. In Holmberg's words, "The visual becomes a metaphor for the central teaching goal of the class and 'speaks' with eloquent clarity and cohesion" (p. 20).

The actual visual models developed in the seminars ranged from an artistic representation of a tree, with key concepts indicated on the branches, to a geometric design of overlapping circles, in which each circle represented a concept central to the course. A visual model for a class in management theory consisted of a linear formula illustrating the concepts and variables involved in analyzing a management problem. Another visual model resembled the "before and after" advertisements for weight loss or body building. Developed by a teacher of statistics, it showed what she thought students' thought processes when analyzing raw data looked like before the students took her course and what she hoped these processes would look like when the course was over. Examples of participants' visual models are shown in Figures 2, 3, and 4.

Not all attempts at visualization were successful. One professor, who was having a difficult time communicating with students in his philosophy of religion class, despaired of visually representing the critical thinking skills he wanted students to learn. He did, however, offer the group a graphic verbal representation of the general direction his class took. He said, "At the beginning of this course I envision myself and my students entering a ship for a grand journey into new realms of thought. We set sail, and somewhere about the fourth week of class the ship sinks." Such humor often saved participants from taking themselves too seriously.

It should not be surprising that many teachers found the creation of visual models far more helpful than written or verbal exercises as a means of understanding their own thinking processes. Such a result is entirely consistent with Piaget's theory that all learning begins in concrete experience before progressing to an abstract representation, a theory we will explore in more depth in the next chapter. In order to make the implicit framework of their mental process explicit, they had to begin, just as their students did, with something concrete—a visual representation.

Of course, we can never fully comprehend what goes on in our brains when we engage in critical thinking. Yet making

Figure 2. Visual Model of Factors Affecting Children.

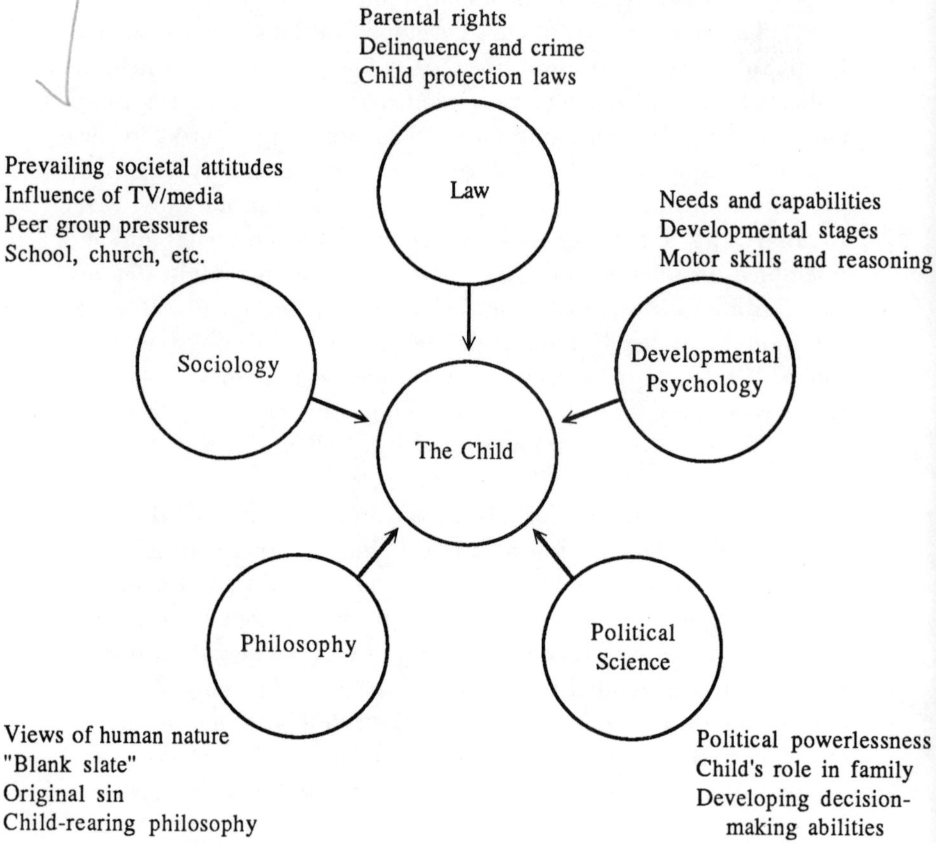

This visual model was developed by a faculty member for her seminar "Children in American Society." The seminar is interdisciplinary and attempts to provide a framework for students to understand the different forces that impinge upon and define the role and status of children in today's family and in American society at large. The model lists only a few of the conceptual considerations under each discipline.

explicit even an approximation of that complex thought process is helpful to students trying to learn its rudiments. Indeed, the great value of a visual model is that it does simplify an incredibly complex process. This simplification can greatly aid students in

Figure 3. Visual Model of Managerial Problem Solving.

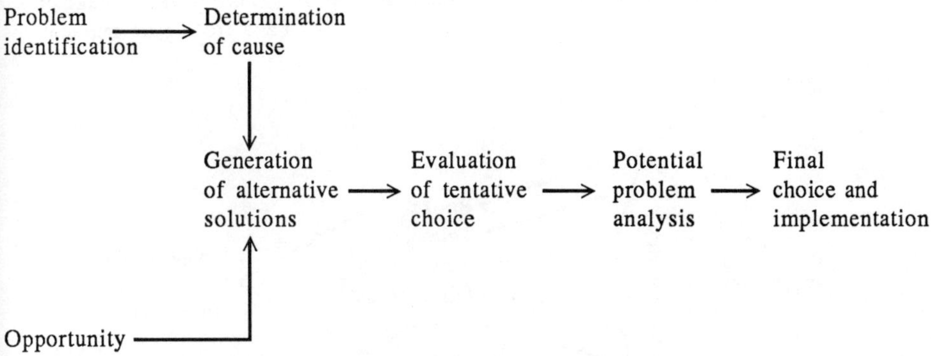

This model was designed by a member of a business faculty for his course "Managerial Problem Solving and Decision Making." Courses of this nature, which focus explicitly on a method of problem solving, are easier to create visual models for than most humanities or social science courses.

beginning to grasp the new ways of thinking that their teachers wish them to understand.

Some caveats about the use of visual models in teaching critical thinking are in order, however. The teaching of such models should never become an end in itself, nor should students be required to adhere to a model rigidly. Whatever models are presented will—and should—be modified by students in the creation of their own developing disciplinary perspectives. Furthermore, the attitudes that accompany the teaching of a model are as important as the model itself. The most graphic of models will count for little if its presentation is not accompanied by the fostering of attitudes of questioning, probing, and wonder.

Finally, teachers must be realistic about what can be accomplished in the way of critical thinking development in a typical ten-week college course. Most students' previous thinking processes are not going to be radically altered in this length of time. One can only hope to sketch the "bare bones" of an analytical framework—and even this will not help much until

Figure 4. Visual Model of Critical Thinking in a Philosophy Course.

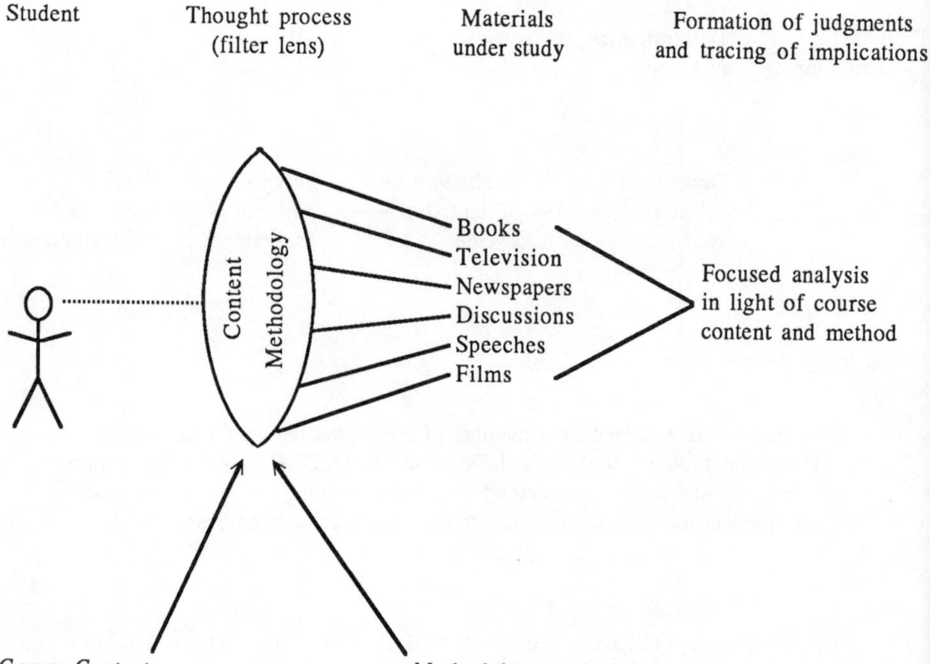

Course Content

Philosophical issues

- Source of truth
- Body/Mind/Spirit
- Good/Evil
- Learned/Innate behavior
- Free will/Determinism
- Optimism/Pessimism
- Human/Animal nature

Methodology and Skills

1. Summarizing what is being said or portrayed
2. Identifying the philosophical issues at stake
3. Recognizing point of view explicit or implicit in materials being studied and illustrating with an example (making and supporting judgments)
4. Drawing conclusions--What are the implications of such a view of human nature?
5. Personal clarification--How does student personally feel about the view being expressed?

This model was developed by a humanities professor for an introductory philosophy class, "Views of Human Nature in Western Culture." The seven issues listed under "Course content" are used to introduce different philosophical views. The methodology items are used throughout the course as formats for both discussion and student assignments or papers.

students have had time to explore the materials of their discipline and realize their need to develop new ways of thinking in order to make sense of this new information.

Helping students recognize this need for change involves challenging their present, often simple, thought processes and then leading them to more abstract and critical levels of thought. In the chapter that follows, we will describe the movement from concrete to abstract thought and present some ways to bring about that movement in the classroom.

3

Developing Students' Capacities for Abstract Thought

When critical thinking is considered in terms of disciplinary perspectives or frameworks for problem solving or analysis and certain attitudes of reflective thought, it follows that the biggest barriers to teaching critical thinking are often students' present attitudes and perspectives. Students do not come to college as blank slates, eagerly awaiting teachers' impressions upon their intellects. They have long since begun to formulate their own perceptions, attitudes, and methods of problem solving. During the college years, it is inevitable and essential that these attitudes and modes of thinking be challenged.

Learning to think critically involves expanding one's thinking processes by moving beyond naturally egocentric attitudes and perceptions and the immediacy of concrete experience. When individuals are in their late teens or early twenties, their modes of thinking are usually based on limited life experience and exposure to a limited set of values and beliefs. One of the biggest challenges for college teachers is helping students broaden their range of experience and exposing them to new values and modes of perception. The abilities to make sense of new experiences and to envision possibilities outside one's own immediate experiences are important ingredients of critical thinking.

We might like to think that by the time students reach college age they have developed some ability to step back from their own values and beliefs, but it takes little experience in college teaching to realize this is not usually the case. The college freshman who quickly assumes that Plato's view of the universe is wrong, simply because it does not conform to her own values and assumptions, lives in a rather constricted universe. Similarly, the student who parrots a limited perception of capitalism and whose main criticism of socialism is that it encourages laziness and sloth is too stuck in his own values and perceptions to engage in much critical thinking.

To engage in what John Dewey called "reflective thought"—to suspend judgment, maintain a healthy skepticism, and exercise an open mind—requires a fair degree of maturity. One of the primary aims of college education is to move students from a self-centered universe, based on limited personal experiences and concrete realities, to a richer, more abstract, realm where a multiplicity of values, visions, and verities exists. Students cannot learn to think critically until they can, at least momentarily, set aside their own visions of the truth and reflect on alternatives. As part of this process, students must be taught to *abstract from* their own immediate experiences in such a way as to expand their thinking abilities.

Moving from Concrete Experience to Abstraction

One definition of abstract thinking is the ability to identify principles or concepts in specific experiences that can be generalized to other experiences. Thinking abstractly also implies some degree of objectivity—the ability to step back from one's own values and beliefs and, at least momentarily, suspend judgment. One of the thornier problems in college teaching is figuring out how to help students get some distance from their own values and beliefs so that they can entertain more abstract modes of perception.

Piaget's (1964) theory of thought structures offers a framework for understanding how abstract thought develops from concrete experience. In his four-stage model of intellectual development, children move from an egocentric world, where they deal primarily in concrete personal experiences, to a less self-centered world, where they begin to focus outside themselves, to conceptualize abstractly, and to entertain alternative possibilities and modes of perceptions. As children move through these stages, their structures of thought increase in both number and complexity.

Piaget's first two stages need not concern us, for they involve very young children. Consideration of the last two stages of intellectual development described by his theory, however, can offer valuable insights into the development of abstract thought and the teaching of critical thinking.

Between the ages of six and eleven, children begin to generalize and categorize. They not only learn to distinguish between, say, the classifications *dog* and *cat* but become able to recognize beagles, cocker spaniels, poodles, and so on, as subclassifications of dogs. At this stage, children also learn the rudiments of mathematics and quantification. Piaget calls this stage *concrete-operational.* The term *concrete* is used because the child's mental structures relate to a visible, tangible world of immediate experiences, and not to verbally stated hypotheses (Lawson and Renner, 1975, p. 341). The word *operational* refers to the types of operations or structures that the child can utilize. In this stage, the child learns to use some of the basic tools of logical reasoning but still has difficulty in dealing with verbal or written abstractions. Thus, a child may not comprehend the general applicability of the abstraction *ecosystem* but can understand the specifics of how guppies interact in the limited biological community of an aquarium.

In the final, *formal-operational,* stage of development (ages eleven to sixteen), Piaget believes, children develop the ability to abstract from concrete experience and shift their focus from tangible realities to the realm of possibility. At this stage, a child is "capable of reasoning with verbal elements alone, and there is no need for objects" (Lawson and Renner, 1975, p. 341). In Piaget's words, the child can now reason hypothetically (Piaget, 1964, p. 173). In our example, a child in this stage can not only comprehend the abstraction *ecosystem* and see how it applies to other examples, such as a deer in a pine forest, but can even envision fantasy ecosystems. This ability to entertain alternatives is at the heart of learning to think critically—the ability to formulate generalizations, entertain new possibilities, and suspend judgment.

Research suggests that Piaget's assumption that most children can operate at fairly abstract levels by the age of sixteen is a bit optimistic. Some researchers, using Piaget's own testing methods, have shown that a significant percentage of entering college freshmen are not functioning at formal or abstract levels of thought (Kolodiy, 1975; Tomlinson-Keasey, 1972). My own experience with adult students has convinced me that, even at the age of thirty-five, many adults still function as concrete thinkers in some areas of thought. (Piaget did not conceive of the movement from concrete to abstract thought as being uniform. It is quite possible for a student to be operating at a fairly abstract level in one academic discipline or area of study while still functioning at a concrete level in other areas.)

Piaget did not use the word *critical* in his discussion of mental operations, but there are obvious parallels between his category of formal or abstract thought and what we have defined as critical thinking—that is, the abilities to formulate generalizations, entertain new possibilities, and suspend judgment.

Of course, Piaget's entire developmental model is open to question. It is obvious that his logical-scientific bias is a product of Western thought, and studies have pointed out a cultural bias in his methodology (Ashton, 1978). Nonetheless, much can be learned from his model of intellectual development. Whatever terms are used, most teachers recognize some truth in Piaget's description of the way students expand their perceptions of the world and begin thinking abstractly. His description of the movement from concrete reasoning, based on limited life experiences, to more abstract modes of thinking provides some very practical guidelines for the teaching of critical thinking.

The key to the movement from concrete to abstract is the order of this movement: concrete experience first, then abstraction. This idea may seem like mere common sense—but it stands in direct opposition to traditional teaching methods, which introduce abstractions first and then seek to have students confirm those abstractions through some concrete method of verification. In traditional science courses, for example, the theoretical aspects of the subject are almost always presented in class lectures or textbooks before the students reenact or confirm the theories in a laboratory. Similarly, in humanities courses, teachers normally introduce concepts, themes, or generalizations first and then have students find examples of them in primary source materials. In other words, traditional teaching rehearses students in the confirmation of abstractions, not their discovery.

With such an approach, it is little wonder that classroom atmospheres are often stultifying. By presenting abstractions first, teachers rob students of the pleasure of discovery. Kinney (1980) calls the teaching of abstractions in an artificial context, devoid of any association with the world as students know it, "disembedded learning." Learning *how* to "disembed" or dig out the general from the specific is central to abstract thinking, but teachers should not shortcut that process for students by teaching abstractions in and of themselves. Instead, they should create a problem-solving atmosphere that engages students' interest and provides motivation to discover the process of abstract thinking. Kinney states, "Teachers should spend time explaining the problem and devise teaching strategies that do not allow students to think they are being asked to perform outside a meaningful context but place them at the center of expanding concentric circles" (p. 7). As those "expanding concentric circles" move away from limited, ego-centered views of the universe, students will develop the abstract reasoning abilities that are the hallmark of an educated person.

Adapting the basic tenets of Piaget's learning theory to classroom teaching requires the creation of an *active* learning environment. In this environment, students formulate their own questions, problems, and hypotheses rather than simply being passive receptors of knowledge. They begin by exploring and experimenting with materials, objects, and concrete experiences and then move toward the understanding of abstract concepts or principles. For example, students might experiment with inclined planes, read *Moby Dick,* study the *Federalist Papers,* or examine a marketing questionnaire—and *then* ask the question "What's going on here?"

With the teacher's help, concrete problems involving the materials of a discipline can create the disequilibrium necessary for the development of abstract modes of thinking. As Lawson and

Renner suggest, "It is the experience with the materials of the discipline that produces the person who can understand abstract content, and not studying abstract content that produces students who can interact with the materials and invent abstract generalizations" (1975, p. 338).

Interactions among students are also an important part of the struggle to move from concrete to abstract thought. Confronting questions and conclusions of fellow students, often different from one's own, adds to the disequilibrium that helps to shake students from their egocentric perceptions of the world. The teacher may guide the questioning toward the concepts or abstractions that eventually will be taught, but students should be made to understand that being correct or incorrect is not so important as the ability to perceive a problem and wrestle with it. The use of classroom interactions to develop abstract thought will be discussed further in Chapter Five.

The Learning Cycle Approach

One of the pioneers in applying Piaget's learning theory to specific classroom experiences is Robert Karplus, former dean of the graduate school at the University of California at Berkeley. Although Karplus's initial educational training was in physics, he had also studied Piaget. Because many of Piaget's early experiments with children focused on mental operations relevant to physics—conservation of volume, reversibility of order, and so on—it was not surprising that Karplus would decide to adopt some of Piaget's theories in his work with elementary school students.

Karplus and his associates experimented with ways to apply Piaget's concept of the movement from concrete to abstract levels of thought to their classroom activities. They developed a simple three-stage "learning cycle" that incorporated exploration of materials and the introduction of new concepts (Karplus and others, 1978). Their work was so successful with young children that they adapted it to college teaching. Karplus originally created learning cycles for use in laboratory sessions with science students, but soon teachers in the humanities and social sciences also began developing learning cycles for their disciplines.

The purpose of the learning cycle is to involve students in the exploration of experiments or discipline-related problems in order to arouse their curiosity and thereby lead them to abstract levels of thought. We will examine the learning cycle's three stages briefly here.

The first stage involves the *exploration of materials.* Before any exploration begins, the teacher must identify clearly the key concepts or principles to be taught. The teacher then carefully selects materials that relate to those concepts and are relatively familiar to students. Students begin working with these materials, discussing their explorations with other students and the teacher. The most important aspect of this part of the learning cycle is the creation of an atmosphere in which probing, puzzling, and raising questions provide a natural challenge to the students' present mental structures, thereby creating the disequilibrium necessary for change.

During the exploration phase, the teacher's roles are primarily those of catalyst and facilitator—raising additional questions, offering encouragement, and making sure that exploration begins to lead in the direction of the abstractions he or she intends to teach.

In the second stage, *invention of concepts,* the teacher helps the students use their interactions with materials and the questions arising from those interactions as a point of departure for introducing generalizations, principles, or concepts that will make sense of the original explorations. Through this process, students are gently led to understand abstractions in a meaningful context. If necessary, teachers may introduce additional experiences or information to aid in the formulation of new mental structures.

This part of the learning cycle is usually the most challenging and frustrating to teachers. They must not rush to draw conclusions for students but rather let students struggle with the trial and error and the discomfort involved in developing new ways of thinking.

In the final phase of the learning cycle, *application of concepts,* students apply the concepts, principles, or generalizations they have just formulated to work with a new but related set of materials. The purpose of this phase is to reinforce the newly developed mental structures. The teacher here assumes the role of mentor. He or she supports students as they test their abilities to apply newly developed abstractions to new situations.

A simple example of a learning cycle in biology might be the development of the concept *biological community*. Students might observe the interactions of fish, plants, snails, water, light, and food in an aquarium. From their observations, they could formulate such questions as "How do plants grow?" "How do plants and fish interact?" "What role does the aquarium light play in this community?" The teacher might also encourage the students to introduce different species of fish in order to observe a predator-prey relationship. This might lead to the question "Why do some fish feed on simple life forms (simulated by fish food), while others feed on small fish?" During this stage of exploration, students would be encouraged to collect data based on their observations.

During the invention phase, students would be asked to hypothesize about all the different interactions taking place in the aquarium ecosystem. Here the teacher could help students see relationships between various variables—light and plants, plants and fish, food and fish, food and plants, plants and oxygen. Once the overall concept, *biological community,* has been invented, students could go on to develop related concepts, such as *oxygen cycle, nutrient cycle,* and *food chain.*

Finally, in the application phase, students might be asked to apply their newly discovered abstractions to a larger biological community, such as a freshwater pond or ocean, or a terrestrial community, such as a hardwood forest.

The learning cycle approach was first used in the physical sciences, but its application to other disciplines is obvious. A teacher of modern literature might want to build a learning cycle around the concept of the tragic hero or heroine, for example. During the exploration phase, students might read *Oedipus Rex* and develop questions about what is going on in the play and what the concept *tragic* means. This exploration might involve only one or two classroom sessions. During the next few sessions, students might read a different work, such as *Billy Budd,* while the teacher, using the questions from *Oedipus,* helps them develop and expand on some of the common themes of tragedy. In the application phase, students might read a short modern work, such as *Hedda Gabler,* and analyze this work in light of the concepts of tragedy they have developed, comparing and contrasting the new work with *Oedipus* and *Billy Budd.*

The development of learning cycles in the humanities is particularly challenging, for, while the sciences have a long tradition of teaching critical thinking by means of a fairly specific methodology, no such tradition exists in the humanities. The relative lack of learning cycle models in the humanities can be a blessing, however, for it allows teachers to create a multiplicity of models. Readers interested in detailed examples of learning cycles in both the humanities and the sciences are referred to *Multidisciplinary Piagetian-Based Programs for College Freshmen,* published by the University of Nebraska at Lincoln (Fuller, 1977).

The ADAPT Program and Project SOAR

One of the largest and most successful implementations of the Karplus learning cycle in college teaching is the ADAPT (Accent on Developing Abstract Processes of Thought) program at the University of Nebraska's Lincoln campus. The stated purposes of the program are to provide a strong foundation in a variety of disciplines and to encourage students to think logically and critically (Fuller, 1977, p. 120). Entering freshmen may volunteer to enroll in the ADAPT curriculum, which involves taking seven courses in a variety of disciplines. In recent years, the disciplines were anthropology, energy (physics), economics, literature, mathematics, sociology, and computer science. All the ADAPT courses are based on the learning cycle model.

Robert Fuller has directed the ADAPT program since its inception in 1975. Faculty participating in the program were selected from a group of volunteers interested in focusing their teaching on the development of student thinking abilities. Initially the group studied Piaget's theory and the Karplus learning cycle.

Then they worked together to develop and critique learning cycles for specific courses in their various disciplines.

ADAPT has been functioning for thirteen years, at this writing. Although it is often difficult to measure the success of such ventures, students enrolled in the ADAPT program do seem to have shown major gains in critical thinking abilities. ADAPT uses (among other instruments) the Watson-Glaser Critical Thinking Appraisal Test to measure logical and critical thinking. Pretest and posttest results were compared for ADAPT students and two control groups. ADAPT students were found to have improved as much as one standard deviation over the control groups in critical thinking abilities (Fuller, 1977, pp. 120–130).

One strength of the ADAPT program is the sense of community that develops among its students, who make up a small group in a large and often impersonal university. These students not only take the same courses but experience a unifying methodology in those courses, regardless of subject matter. Another major accomplishment of the program has been the development of learning cycles in disciplines outside the sciences. As a result of ADAPT's success, teachers at other colleges have been encouraged to explore the "discovery" mode of teaching and to develop learning cycle models in a variety of academic disciplines. Though the ADAPT program remains small, it continues to grow and proves the viability of teaching students to think critically by improving their abstract reasoning abilities.

Another successful implementation of the learning cycle model has been achieved at Xavier University of Louisiana, a small, predominantly black institution located in New Orleans. Over 40 percent of its student body pursues natural, mathematical, or health sciences majors. Although Xavier is fairly small, with an enrollment of fewer than 1,600, only three schools in the entire country—Harvard, Michigan, and Howard—sent more blacks into medical training in 1981 (Carmichael, 1982). Many factors account for Xavier's success, but a major share of that success can be attributed to Project SOAR (Stress on Analytical Reasoning).

SOAR is a five-week summer training program for students who will enter Xavier formally as freshmen the following fall. Like the ADAPT program, SOAR is based on Piagetian theory and the Karplus learning cycle. The format for the learning cycles is quite different at SOAR, however, because they must be collapsed into a shorter block of time and are therefore much more intensive. During the five-week program, students spend their mornings in small groups focusing on five abstract aspects of general problem solving that are of particular concern to science students. These include controlling variables, probabilistic reasoning, proportional reasoning, combinational reasoning, and recognizing correlations. These abstractions are "discovered" by students in three-hour laboratory sessions where they are free to explore, invent, and apply new modes of thinking. Each concept is presented in the context of five different disciplines—biology, chemistry, computer science, mathematics, and physics. By the end of the five weeks, therefore, students have had the opportunity to use the same abstraction in five different settings, thereby providing a firm foundation for the development of an analytical framework in the sciences.

In the afternoons, SOAR students depart from the learning cycle format and spend their time in small groups working to improve verbal abilities, such as vocabulary, note taking, and logical problem solving. An interesting aspect of the afternoon sessions is the approach taken to logical problem solving. SOAR students work with upperclassmen from Xavier in attempting to solve assigned problems from a workbook by "thinking aloud." First the SOAR students attempt to solve a problem; then an experienced student works through the same problem. As we noted in Chapter Two, thinking aloud is one good way to describe explicitly the steps that individuals go through in analysis and problem solving. The SOAR *Problem Solving and Comprehension* workbook states, "In contrast to playing golf, analyzing complex material is an activity which is generally done inside your head. This makes it difficult for a teacher to teach and a learner to learn. In other words, a beginner cannot observe how an expert thinks and solves problems. . . . In this way the steps they have taken are open to view; their activities can be observed and communicated" (Whimbey and Lochhead, 1979, p. 27).

The combination of "thinking aloud" and learning cycle labs seems to help students improve their critical thinking abilities. Tests on an instrument designed by Piagetian scholar Anton Lawson to measure the development of formal reasoning skills have indicated that three-fourths of the students tested obtained significantly higher scores at the end of the SOAR program than they did at the beginning. Data from the Nelson-Denny Reading Test (reading comprehension and vocabulary) showed average increases in scores ranging from 1.8 grade levels (for those below or equal to the twelfth-grade level on the pretest) to 2.2 grade levels (for those below the tenth-grade level on the pretest). Testing on the Preliminary Scholastic Aptitude Test revealed similar gains in verbal and reading comprehension scores (Whimbey and others, 1980).

Assets and Limitations of Learning Cycle Models

Two major assumptions underlie the learning cycle approach to teaching. The first is that teachers must know the essentials of what they want students to learn: Each course must be stripped down to the basic nub. For this reason, it may take as much time to identify goals and prepare a learning cycle as it does to actually teach one. Teachers must also expect to teach a given cycle a number of times before all the kinks are worked out of it.

A second important consideration is that enough time must be set aside to fully engage students in the various activities involved in a cycle. This can cause definite problems for teachers who have to follow a traditional fifty-minute class structure. Learning cycles are much more successful when classes can last an hour and a half to three hours.

One advantage of the learning cycle approach is that it can be used in a number of ways. As in the ADAPT program, it can provide the framework for an entire ten- or twelve-week college course. In a ten-week course, the first three weeks might be used in exploration, the next four in invention and introduction of concepts, and the final three in application of concepts to new materials. For teachers considering the development of a course-long learning cycle, the Karplus workshop guide, *Science Teaching and the Development of Reasoning* (1978), is extremely helpful. To identify overall teaching goals and the structure of the critical thinking process one wants students to learn, teachers might try the visualization technique described in Chapter Two. In Chapter Eight, we will consider a seminar for faculty development that is helpful in conceptualizing overall learning cycle goals.

Learning cycles can also be used in short-term teaching activities, such as the three-hour science labs in the SOAR program. Here the focus is less on the development of an overall process of critical thinking and more on the development of key concepts. I have experimented with using "minicycles" in my philosophy courses, which have a three-hour class format, by focusing each class on one or two key philosophical concepts. Sometimes I use films or newspaper or magazine articles to introduce the concept. Students observe a film or read an article and then spend fifteen to twenty minutes raising questions, developing hypotheses, and challenging each other. This process almost always generates a lot of discussion, debate, and enthusiasm. Then we try to develop a consensus on our conclusions. During this time I share with students the ways I perceived the film or article and follow this with a formal introduction of the concepts for that day. Exploration and invention are thus accomplished in one class period. In the class following, I give students a brief newspaper article that relates to the concepts covered in the previous class and ask them to apply what they have learned to the new material.

Because of time pressure, use of the learning cycle approach almost always creates tension between the delivery of content and the teaching of the critical thinking process. It takes time for students to struggle with materials and develop their own questions and hypotheses. Teachers who have used learning cycles report that they often have to pare down their normal content presentations by as much as one-third or one-half. As a result, they express some concern—and experience some guilt—about "short-changing" students by not covering traditional amounts of course content. Most feel, however, that these losses are outweighed by seeing students make dramatic improvements in their thinking abilities.

Using the learning cycle approach also has radical implications for the ways most of us function as teachers. In theory a learning cycle sounds exciting, but implementing one can be difficult. During the first few times I taught my minicycles, my biggest frustration was my own inability to remain silent and let students struggle. It took a lot of energy to bridle my tongue. I inevitably rushed to draw a conclusion before most students had even grasped the problem. Using learning cycles requires giving students time to reflect, and reflection often involves silence. I'm not sure who is more uncomfortable with silence in the classroom, me or my students—but I do know, from actually timing myself, that five seconds of silence seems interminable. Teachers using learning cycles will find themselves spending most of their class time as referees, coaches, and mentors rather than as lecturers and purveyors of the truth. For most of us, this is a worthwhile but difficult shift.

Of course, learning cycles are only one of many approaches to the teaching of critical thinking. Piaget's learning theory can be applied to the classroom in other ways, and other theories can be substituted for Piaget's. Nonetheless, Piaget's basic insights about how individuals learn to think abstractly—particularly his insights regarding mental structures and operations, the role of disequilibrium, and the necessity for questions and discovery—seem valid to me.

Students will move beyond their limited, immediate experience and develop new mental structures for critical thinking only when their present structures are insufficient to the task at hand and when an atmosphere of discovery encourages them to explore new modes of thinking. In the next chapter we will consider some simple and practical ways to capture student interest and set them on the road to discovery. We will also discuss the use of analogy and related techniques to bridge the chasm that often exists between concrete and abstract patterns of thought.

4

Fostering Student Interest and Motivation

"There can be no mental development without interest. Interest is the *sine qua non* for attention and apprehension. You may endeavor to excite interest by means of birch rods, or you may coax it by the incitement of pleasurable activity. But without interest there will be no progress" (Whitehead, [1929] 1967, p. 37).

Alfred North Whitehead's words address one of the most essential, yet elusive, elements in teaching—student interest and motivation. They are disconcerting words, for they remind teachers how powerless they are over what is going on in their students' minds during classroom hours. One can have complete mastery of a given subject, know the exact nature of the disciplinary perspective or critical thinking framework to be taught, and lecture and lead discussion with great sensitivity and élan. But if student interest is not present, all is for naught.

This point was brought home to me recently when a colleague invited me to sit in on one of her literature classes. Sitting in the last row of students, observing the class interactions, was a revealing experience. My colleague did a fine job in presenting her lecture, and a number of students were listening attentively and taking notes. But an equal number were pursuing other interests. The student to my left was engrossed in writing a letter to a friend. The young woman directly in front of me was busy reading and taking notes for what looked like an upcoming exam in Spanish. Two students in the next row were passing notes back and forth. And, during the five minutes before the class ended, fully half of the class turned to check the clock on the back wall.

My experience was not an isolated one. Most teachers are painfully aware of the low level of student attention. But why should this be so? Cognitive theorists assure us that children have a natural sense of exploration and wonder. Indeed, to some degree, all animals probably possess innate curiosity. The philosopher Michael Polanyi writes, "As far down the scale of life as worms and even perhaps amoebas, we meet a general alertness of animals, not directed towards any specific satisfaction, but merely exploring what is there: an urge to achieve intellectual control over the situations confronting [them]" (1962, p. 132). Polanyi goes on to cite experiments demonstrating the apparent pleasure that chimpanzees derive from the discovery of new ways to manipulate simple tools (p. 133).

Why do these positive assessments of human beings and "lower" life forms contrast so dramatically with many experiences of college teachers? Where is that childlike sense of wonder, inquisitiveness, and playfulness in a group of passive college students, almost daring a teacher to spark their interest in philosophy or literature? Shouldn't we expect at least as much interest from students as chimpanzees exhibit?

Barriers to Student Interest

Optimistic assessments of human curiosity and despairing visions of stone-faced college students are equally true. Human beings are born with an innate curiosity and sense of wonder, but these must be nurtured if they are to survive. It is no accident that the most positive perceptions of human learning capabilities come from those who have worked with children and adults in highly supportive and individualized environments. Indeed, the Piagets and Montessoris of the world struggled to create flexible, supportive environments precisely because they were so aware that the natural inclination to learn must be nurtured. All too often, the family, school, and larger society do not provide students with this kind of environment.

To understand why college students often exhibit less than encouraging levels of interest, we need look no further than two general predispositions that many students bring with them from previous socialization and schooling: an attitude of intellectual passivity or disengagement, and negative preconceptions about academic disciplines. As Carl Sagan observes, "I think everybody is born with wonder, and that society beats it out of you. . . . Youngsters who are slowly examining the world around them and wondering about it ask perfectly good questions, like, 'Why is the grass green?' because they can envision it purple, or orange. . . . The adult who is answering the question is annoyed . . . and says, 'Don't ask dumb questions. What color do you expect it to be?'" (Sweeney, 1982, p. B7).

Not all adults are as insensitive as Sagan's caricature, but our culture does exert pressure on children to remain silent and follow instructions rather than asking questions. Thus, natural inquisitiveness is soon replaced by passivity and a tendency to take cues from others. Children learn to forgo their own questions and answers and, instead, ask the kinds of questions and provide the kinds of answers they think teachers and other adults want to hear. By the time most students reach college age, the inner-directed child has become the other-directed young adult. Passivity and caution have replaced inquisitiveness and questioning, and taking notes on the thoughts of others has replaced thinking for oneself.

Other pressures, inherent in the very structure of the traditional public school day, also encourage intellectual caution and discourage reflective thinking. It is difficult to nurture natural interests and encourage attitudes of reflection when students are never given enough time to become fully involved with a subject. Elkind (1978) suggests that by the time most students reach the third or fourth grade, their natural inquisitiveness has already been discouraged, if not actually impaired, by a schooling process that constantly shuttles them back and forth between different activities every hour on the hour.

Indeed, one could scarcely envision a system better designed to impede interest and discourage critical inquiry than the traditional fifty-minute to hour-long class format used by most grade schools, high schools, and colleges. It takes time for anyone to settle down and become seriously engaged in a topic of interest. Such engagement is well nigh impossible in an environment where a new topic, teacher, or both are introduced every hour and there is no time between classes to process and reflect on what was just studied. To cope with the demands of this constant barrage of competing subjects, students learn to disengage their intellectual capacities. Indeed, traditional schooling almost requires disengagement. By the ripe old age of nine or ten, most youngsters have learned well the lesson that school is not the place to get any serious thinking done.

A second barrier that impedes interest and motivation is composed of the negative preconceptions students often bring to the study of particular academic disciplines. Some of these attitudes may result from previous encounters with poor teachers, while others may arise from students' own idiosyncratic likes or dislikes, over which teachers have no control. For example, as a teacher of philosophy, I am well aware of the negative preconceptions that many students bring to this subject. If a student really thinks of philosophy, as one student put it, as "a bunch of old men in tweed suits, sitting around smoking their pipes and spouting irrelevancies," then my work is obviously cut out for me.

More is required to combat these preconceptions than merely beginning each new class with a disclaimer—"Now, I know a lot of you think philosophy (or any discipline) is a lot of bunk, but. . . ." A better approach is to take some time at the start of each semester to ask students what value they perceive a given discipline to have in the context of their lives. Opening such a dialogue provides an opportunity to acknowledge negative preconceptions and to share with students some of the reasons why the teacher thinks his or her discipline is important.

Anonymous survey forms provide one simple and efficient means of ascertaining student attitudes. These forms may be distributed, completed, and collected at the beginning of the first class session. They require only ten minutes to administer and can provide a wealth of information to help teachers stimulate student interest, including attitudes or misconceptions about a discipline, personal objectives for taking a course, previous coursework in the discipline or a related one, and areas of individual or group interest. Students should be told how the survey information will be used, so that they will take the exercise seriously. Survey findings may be summarized and shared with students at the following class as a means of initiating discussion. Exhibits 1 and 2 show examples of survey forms.

Survey forms allow students to express their preconceptions and apprehensions. When instructors openly acknowledge these attitudes, the classroom can take on an atmosphere of candor and reality that fosters critical thinking and stimulates interest. Learning to think critically in any discipline begins with an appreciation of the value of a disciplinary perspective. Teachers must not *assume* that appreciation, however, but *create* it. Unless we can combat students' negative preconceptions by showing them the usefulness of our disciplinary perspectives in their own lives, there is little hope that they will become interested enough to attempt adopting them.

Encouraging Student Interest: Problems and Wonder

One way to begin encouraging inquisitive and reflective habits of mind is to create a learning environment that partakes of the mysterious. In a provocative article, "The Art of Teaching Science," biologist Lewis Thomas urges teachers to abandon old modes of instruction that assume that what needs to be communicated is a body of factual knowledge. Rather than introducing students to terminology, basic concepts, and underlying laws, he suggests beginning every course by telling them some of the things scientists do *not* understand. "Let it be known early on, that there are deep mysteries and profound paradoxes. . . . Describe as clearly as possible . . . that there are some things going on in the universe that lie still beyond our comprehension, and make it plain how little is known" (Thomas, 1982, p. 92).

In other words, begin each course with something that is a problem or a cause for wonder. Set students' minds to pondering, for in such a context they will experience both curiosity to know more and disequilibrium that will challenge their old ways of thinking and prepare them for new modes of critical thinking.

Thomas's advice to science teachers could well be applied by teachers in any discipline. Humanities teachers are in as much danger of merely presenting the critics' interpretations of Shakespeare, the "appropriate" way to analyze a Van Gogh painting, or

Exhibit 1. "Counseling Theories and Techniques": Student Survey Form.

During the next ten weeks we will look at a number of different approaches to counseling. Please complete this form to enable me to better choose assigned readings and other learning strategies.

Indicate any courses or workshops you have taken that relate to counseling or human services (for example, psychology, family studies, sociology, interpersonal communications, group dynamics).

Indicate work or volunteer experiences you have had that involve counseling or human services.

What are some of your conceptions and/or opinions about people who use counseling in their line of work?

Below are a number of different approaches to counseling. Please circle on the rating scale how familiar you are with their terminology, concepts, or theorists.

Approach	Very familiar				Not at all familiar
Client-centered	5	4	3	2	1
Rational-emotive	5	4	3	2	1
Adlerian	5	4	3	2	1
Reality	5	4	3	2	1
Gestalt	5	4	3	2	1
Behavioral psychology	5	4	3	2	1
Psychoanalysis	5	4	3	2	1

Exhibit 2. "Case Studies in American History": Student Survey Form.

---

1. If you had a history course in high school or previous college work on history, what did the courses cover? Say a few words about what you liked or disliked about these courses.

2. What do you think historians do?

3. Name one historical event you feel was important. Explain briefly why this event was important.

4. Recently the journal of a pioneer woman was discovered in north central Minnesota. It dates from about the mid 1850s. What possible benefit could this journal be to historians?

---

the "real" causes and interpretations of the Civil War as chemistry instructors are of dwelling on the "laws" of chemistry. After all, who actually knows what Shakespeare or Van Gogh intended? Does anyone understand the "real" causes and interpretations of an historical event? Teachers must convince students that their disciplines contain unresolved questions and issues worthy of pondering if they want them to have motivation to develop critical analytical skills.

By modeling reflective thought in lectures and discussion, teachers can do much to encourage this frame of mind in their students. Teachers give a personal cast to critical thinking when they initiate courses with topics or issues *they* consider to be problems. Students need to know that their teachers do not claim to have all the answers and that finding the "right" answer may not be as important as understanding what is at stake and knowing how to pose relevant questions. In the reflective classroom, both teacher and students will appreciate the fact that some problems may forever remain a mystery.

One practical strategy for demonstrating interesting problems at the beginning of a course is to present to students the opposing views on a major disciplinary issue about which experts of equal stature disagree dramatically. Then ask students how it is possible for experts to come to such different conclusions. For example, I begin a philosophy course on human nature with a film that illustrates how two paleontologists, looking at the same skulls of early humanoids, come to radically different conclusions. One expert tries to prove that humans descended from a line of "killer apes," while the other expert, using the same bones, shows how we must have descended from social, "pastoral" creatures. I use this film to stimulate interest and to "hook" students on my topic. The film never fails to generate discussion, and it creates fertile ground for sowing the seeds of critical skills that students will need to clarify their own views on human nature.

Every discipline lends itself in some way to such an approach. There are opposing theories of mental disease, conflicting interpretations of history, different theories of management. Students in introductory music or art courses usually find it interesting that many great works in these fields were not immediately hailed as triumphs and that experts still disagree about what constitutes "real" art. Presenting a problem or controversy at the beginning of a course forces students to acknowledge a tension or to take a stand on an issue. A wealth of films, filmstrips, and videocassettes are available to set the stage for lively discussion. If one important aspect of critical thinking is problem solving and analysis, it certainly makes sense to begin college courses with a problem.

Matthew Lipman uses a problem-related approach in teaching philosophy to grade school children. He suggests that teachers create materials that contain "intellectual shock and surprise" to catch students' interest (1976, p. 56). "We can hardly expect to arouse real resourcefulness and spontaneity of the student without presenting him striking ideas of some kind. And at the same time we must be prepared to *guide* his resourcefulness so that he can see its rewards, rather than that he should become disenchanted as a result of the fruitlessness of his own ramblings" (p. 28).

Lipman makes the valid point here that guiding student interest is as important as securing it. Simply stimulating interest by presenting a dramatic, "gee whiz" concept or problem is useless unless that interest is subsequently guided by the teaching of ways to analyze or make sense of this subject matter. Unless teachers carefully plan their follow-up, the presentation of exciting ideas and issues may temporarily dazzle students but lead nowhere.

The recommendations of Lipman and Thomas tie in closely with Piaget's concept of disequilibrium and its role in creating motivation to learn new mental structures. Students must first be made both curious and uneasy by presentation of an interesting problem for which no certain answer exists. Then, once interest is captured, they can be guided to learn new modes of thinking and to develop confidence in their ability to analyze and solve problems.

Building on Student Interest: Analogy and Metaphor

After initial interest has been aroused, teachers must begin the ongoing process of encouraging students to raise their own questions and develop their own critical thinking processes. This issue of appropriation—how students make learning their own—is one of the most frustrating concerns in teaching. How do students come to internalize the skills and attitudes of critical thinking, and how can their teachers help them do it?

Piaget, Kohlberg, Perry, and other developmental theorists suggest that the key to appropriation is relating new learning to previous knowledge. Successful leading of students from concrete operations and simple mental structures to more abstract modes of thinking *always* begins by building on past experiences and existing mental structures. Donald Norman argues that "examination of the way in which our students learn indicates that they build upon previous structures. Essentially, they tend to learn by analogy. . . . In order to understand the topic, you have to be able to relate it to other things you know" (1980, p. 44).

In a sense, all learning proceeds from analogy. Indeed, some cognitive scientists suggest that reasoning by analogy is the foundation of all general intelligence (Hunt, 1982). We can understand something new only by recognizing its similarities to and differences from something familiar. If students are introduced to a topic too abstract and far removed from their own experiences and present knowledge, there is little hope they will appropriate it. Thus, a central task of teaching is like bridge building—an analogy itself. Good teachers know how to build connections between the content and methods of their disciplines and students' experiences and concerns.

I still recall a professor from my undergraduate days who was struggling to get our class to understand the function of ritualized magic. He described ritual magic as "the performance of concrete acts that give individuals a sense of mastery over situations in which the outcomes are highly problematical"—a fine example of an academic abstraction. To breathe some life into this arid concept, my professor drew an analogy with the upcoming homecoming dance. He reminded us of television ads for women's lipstick and men's cologne in which dull-looking men and mousy women were magically transformed into irresistible models of glamor by the application of a cosmetic product that all but ensured their success in love. He then talked about the elaborate hygienic rituals that students often went through to prepare for the "big dance." He helped us realize that we engaged in those preparations and used those cosmetics to give ourselves a sense of confidence when heading into the "highly problematical" social situation of the dance. There was no guarantee that the rituals would work, but the very act of engaging in ritual helped to relieve our anxiety.

Suddenly I felt a kinship with the Trobriand Islanders. Just as they daubed their bodies with magical paint before heading out in their tiny canoes to fish the great oceans, I daubed my body with "magical" cologne before facing the uncertainties of the big dance. I have forgotten much of the other content of that sociology course, but the concept of ritualized magic will always be with me.

Analogy is a powerful teaching tool with a long and respected heritage. In Book 2 of his *Rhetoric,* Aristotle describes illustrative parallels (analogies) as one of the three central forms of oratorical argument (McKeon, 1974). There is probably no better way to make an abstract concept come alive and become accessible to students than to use a well-drawn analogy.

Ideas for analogies can come from many sources. For example, the popular media offer a wealth of potential analogical material. An instructor might clip newspaper or magazine articles that illustrate particular concepts studied in class and then ask students to comment on them. Or students can be asked to summarize difficult abstract passages from texts in their own words and to provide illustrations of the concepts from their personal experience. In effect, this approach lets the students themselves become teachers.

A third source of analogies that can be used in teaching is the work of good popular writers. For example, Stephen Jay Gould, noted evolutionary theorist and teacher of biology, geology, and the history of science at Harvard University, is a master of analogy, as can be seen in his popular articles for *Natural History Magazine.* His facility in communicating highly abstract concepts through analogy is evident in his article "A Biological Homage to Mickey Mouse" (1980). In this article, Gould traces the pictorial development of Mickey Mouse from his earliest cartoons, in which his features were fairly sharp and his eyes and skull relatively small, to the cartoons of fifty years later, when his features appear more rounded and his eyes and cranial vault larger. The purpose of this analogy is to illustrate the biological concept of *neoteny,* or the tendency of some animals to retain in their adult stages the juvenile features of their ancestors. Gould goes on to explain that human beings have a preference for juvenile features. Most people prefer rounded, fuzzy, wide-eyed rabbits to sharp, angular, beady-eyed crabs as objects of affection, for example. Using actual caliper measurements, Gould demonstrates Mickey's fifty-year evolution to a more rounded, "lovable" creature. He then argues that Mickey's evolution is no accident but an intentional marketing device of the creative folks at Disney Studios. No doubt there are other ways to help people understand the concept of neoteny, but Gould's analogy is certainly one that most readers will remember.

Analogies offer a fairly direct and obvious way to connect new concepts and ideas to students' previous knowledge. Some concepts, however, cannot be explained by simple, direct comparisons. For these the teacher may turn to metaphor and figurative language. In *Physics as Metaphor,* Roger Jones explains, "Metaphor suggests something more than analogy, for in metaphorical comparison, a new quality or connection is disclosed in the thing compared that was not previously apparent" (1983, p. 51). Jones notes that there is both a passive, comparative aspect to metaphor and an active, creative element that suggests connections between things and hints at deeper meaning (p. 4).

Most of us learned about metaphor in literature classes and therefore tend to assume that its use is restricted to the arts and humanities. However, Jones argues that scientists also use figurative language to clarify their abstract descriptions of reality. For example, astronomers refer to one particularly bewildering galactic feature as a "black hole"—"the perfect metaphor for a bottomless well in space from which not even light may escape" (p. 5).

As described in Chapter Two, visual metaphors can be developed for any discipline. One of my colleagues, a teacher of Eastern religions, uses the metaphor of a wheel and its spokes to help students conceptualize the many paths leading to the same goal in Buddhism. A teacher of American history uses a painting of an angelic spirit guiding the pioneers in their covered wagons over the plains to exemplify the concept of manifest destiny. A professor of counseling theories might use a poetic description of stained glass windows to portray the importance of looking "from the inside out" in order to appreciate a client's problems.

Not all metaphors are visual, however. In her book *Speaking in Parables* (1975), theologian Sally McFague presents a convincing case for the use of stories, parables, and poems as forms of metaphor in teaching. McFague's starting point is concern over the increasingly abstract nature of theological education. She argues that abstract language so separates life from thought that it strangles the life from that which we seek to teach. To enliven the teaching of theology (and, for that matter, any discipline), McFague suggests that teachers draw on the power of various forms of oral metaphor.

McFague defines a metaphor as the use of common words in an unfamiliar context, giving us new insights and moving us "to see the ordinary world in an extraordinary way" (p. 4). The parables of Jesus did just that. Rather than offering abstract discourses on the nature of God and reality, Jesus told stories that used the experiences of everyday life to point to a reality beyond those stories. Similarly, poets paint verbal pictures that point beyond their words. Jesus, Confucius, Emily Dickinson, Studs Terkel, Maya Angelou—prophets, poets, writers—all know how to convey their perceptions of the world through the use of metaphor.

Telling stories is a powerful part of our human heritage. For over a million years, prior to written language, all human wisdom was communicated through stories, tales, and other forms of oral tradition. But storytelling in and of itself is no virtue. There is nothing more boring than a rambling, anecdotally burdened professor telling his or her sad tales. The very power of stories makes it important that they be carefully chosen to teach or illustrate a concept.

Metaphor and analogy are particularly helpful in clarifying certain abstract aspects of critical thinking. Teaching students to think critically involves not so much communicating facts and information as teaching perspectives for analyzing and making sense of information. The figurative language of metaphor and the illustrative force of analogy can help to make those perspectives clear by building bridges from them to things students already know and have experienced. Only by building on their past can we hope to expand students' visions of the future and share with them the contributions we think our respective disciplines can make to that future.

5

Structuring Classes to Promote Critical Thought

Most college teachers would be glad to spend more classroom time engaging student interest, challenging students' present thinking processes, and creating an atmosphere where active reflection and interchange replaces caution and passivity. But the realities of cramped teaching schedules, large class size, limited class time, and voluminous course content militate against most attempts to create such positive learning environments. Teaching the skills and attitudes of critical thinking inevitably necessitates rethinking the role of the teacher as lecturer and reconsidering the amount of classroom time spent teaching content as opposed to the amount spent teaching a process of thought.

Balancing Content and Process

Many of America's earliest colleges were conceived with a dedication to develop certain character traits and habits of thought, but more recently the aims of higher education have drifted toward the mastery of academic content and information. Contemporary American educators have tended to assume that content comes first and thinking processes develop later.

Introductory textbooks usually present basic information and concepts thought to be essential for future study. To be sure, textbook writers often disagree about what the "essential" concepts and information are. Yet both teachers and students often feel obligated to make their way through an entire text at any cost. This frequently leaves little time for anything else. If, in teaching American history, one is expected to "cover" a period stretching from pre-Columbian times to the Civil War in two academic quarters, one will not have much opportunity to worry about whether students are learning to think like historians.

On a philosophical level, of course, one can argue against making a hard-and-fast distinction between content and process. But on a practical level, when sixty minutes of classroom time are at stake, the distinction seems very real. The combination of increased demand for the teaching of critical thinking skills and a flood of new information in most disciplines makes the tension between content and process particularly acute today. Happily, this tension is not so much a case of either/or as a question of priority and balance. Both content and process can be taught, even in limited class time, if proper priorities and balance are maintained. But in striking that balance, teachers must become much more selective in both the content they choose to present and the ways in which they present it.

Whitehead suggested that a "certain ruthless definiteness" should characterize the teaching enterprise and that successful teachers have to know "in precise fashion" what their students need to learn ([1929] 1967, p. 36). His advice is more relevant today than ever before. Unfortunately, since there are no agreed-on guides to determine what content is essential in any discipline, teachers must develop their own.

Posing the question "What do I want students to *know* and what do I want them to be able to *do* by the end of this course?" is one good way to begin paring down a course to its essentials—in other words, working backward from intended outcomes to necessary input. Once central issues and problems are identified, content can be chosen to exemplify and clarify these issues and problems. Trying to visualize the process of critical thinking that teachers intend students to learn (as described in Chapter Two) is another helpful approach to making content decisions. Sharing course objectives and teaching strategies with colleagues is helpful as well. Whatever route is taken, a more conscientious attempt to teach students a process for critical thinking and analysis usually means a dramatic decrease in amounts of content formerly presented.

According to a report from four colleges that created pilot projects to teach critical thinking, most teachers participating in the projects found that they needed to decrease the amount of content covered. Indeed, some reported that they had to cut out as much as 30 to 40 percent of the content they normally lectured on (Fuller, 1977). The faculty participating in the study did, however, report that the reward of seeing students make measurable gains in thinking abilities far outweighed whatever guilt or loss faculty felt for cutting back on content (p. 63).

Some of the inevitable guilt that accompanies this paring down of content can be alleviated by considering how arbitrary the delineation of course content often is. Where is it written that an introductory history course must "cover" a specific span of time? Is one modern literature course better than another because students read seven novels in the one and only three in the other? Even when college department committees agree to adopt one standard text for all survey classes, what guarantee is there that different concepts will not be emphasized by different teachers?

If the major goal of a philosophy class is to have students begin thinking philosophically, for example, it may not be necessary to expose them to an arbitrary quota of great philosophers. The course might be better organized around central concepts, issues, and philosophic questions, with specific philosophers used when and where their contributions apply. But even when teaching is approached in such a thematic manner, teachers must still face the reality that only a limited number of concepts can be communicated to students during a given course. When thinking processes are taught explicitly, content must inevitably be decreased.

Balancing Lecture and Interaction

Previous chapters have emphasized the need for teachers to identify the explicit disciplinary frameworks and processes of critical thinking that they want students to master. But these frameworks and processes are models, nothing more. As students struggle to adopt new modes of thinking, they will inevitably change, adapt, and rework these models. In the last analysis, students must create their own mental structures for critical thinking. Teachers can, however, facilitate that building process by encouraging debate, questioning, and other forms of meaningful student-student and student-teacher interaction in the classroom.

Piaget's learning theory stresses the importance of *social transmission* in the development of new mental structures. Lawson and Renner's comments on the role of social transmission in teaching children also apply to college students. "In order for the learner to be shaken from his egocentric views, he must experience the viewpoints and thoughts of others. . . . If he does not, he has no reason to alter the mental structures that he initially acquired from his self-centered frame of reference. Social interaction can lead to conflict, debate, shared data, and the clear delineation and expression of ideas" (1975, p. 338).

The work of Piaget and developmental theorists like Perry and Kohlberg strongly suggests that active forms of transmission work better than lecture to stimulate cognitive and ethical development in students. This is not to suggest that lecture does not have a proper place in higher education, of course. Lectures are appropriate, perhaps the best, means for stimulating interest by raising questions and presenting problems, providing information not available in texts or supplementary readings, clarifying difficult concepts through example or analogy, summarizing main points of discussion, and demonstrating through example how teachers engage in critical thinking. What is needed is some sort of balance between lecture and interaction. While classroom size may have some impact on the proportions of this balance, meaningful dialogue and discussion can be created in classes of two hundred students, and lecturing to a small seminar group may be quite appropriate at times.

Lecturing is obviously a very comfortable mode of teaching, as witness its long tradition and continued predominance. After all, monologue is much less risky than dialogue. The main problem with lecture as a primary mode of teaching is the disallowance of any time for students to interact with and process subject matter. Furious note taking may appear a form of interaction, but it is no substitute for processing information by thinking out loud, restating concepts in one's own words, discussing issues with fellow students, or challenging a teacher's assumptions and conclusions.

Even the American Medical Association has recently questioned the value of lecture as an exclusive mode of training medical students. A panel on the general professional education of physicians recently issued a report strongly urging medical school faculty to reduce the amount of factual information taught "while increasing the time spent teaching students how to solve problems" (Fields, 1984, p. 15). The panel suggested that in most instances the hours presently spent in medical school lecturing could be reduced by one-third to one-half.

The most brilliant lectures will not foster critical thinking if no time is available for students to raise questions and otherwise respond to those lectures. We must all process information before we can truly make it our own. Such processing requires interaction. A study by Daryl Smith (1977), using both the Watson-Glaser Critical Thinking Appraisal Test and the Chickering Critical Thinking Behaviors Test, demonstrated that student participation, teacher encouragement, and peer interaction correlated positively with improved critical thinking scores. Creating meaningful dialogue and discussion, however, is not simply a matter of providing time for such activities. Planning and forethought are also necessary.

Generating Classroom Discussion

While the advantages of discussion as a means of teaching critical thinking may seem obvious, most teachers are not trained or skilled in the use of dialogue and discussion as teaching tools. Their honest attempts to engage students in dialogue may therefore backfire, reinforcing the very passivity they sought to challenge.

Students often are equally unprepared to engage in meaningful classroom discussion. W. F. Hill writes, "The typical student in our culture has had little preparation for participation in a discussion group, as his academic experience has been dominated by lecture methods. Thus the student and the group flounder and turn to the instructor for help. Due to the instructor's own lack of understanding of group work, or his allegiance to permissivity, he usually cannot or will not provide the training necessary for a productive [discussion] group" (1969, p. 16).

I am reminded of a faculty discussion I overheard recently, in which a professor tried to explain to three peers her attempts to wean herself away from the comforts of lecturing. She related how she had broken her normal hour-long lectures into fifteen-minute segments. At the end of each segment she paused and asked students if there were any questions. Almost inevitably her queries met with silence. Frustrated by the silence, she would then proceed to her next segment. After a few attempts at this new methodology, she abandoned it and returned to her normal lectures. It seemed obvious that this teacher had underestimated both her students' schooling in passivity and the amount of effort she would need to make in order to generate dialogue and interchange.

Merely changing the length of lectures or punctuating them with pauses for questions will seldom generate classroom discussion. This is because students usually interpret a teacher's asking "Are there any questions?" to mean merely "Was my presentation clear?" Any response will thus be an indication that either the teacher has explained something poorly or the student has not understood. Only the most confident student will say anything in such a context. The notion that the teacher really desires dialogue simply will not occur to most class members.

Rather than *ending* presentations with questions, teachers might do better to *begin* each presentation with a question and a brief period of discussion. Beginning with a question creates an atmosphere of anticipation and inquiry. Questions such as "Why does Herman Melville use Ishmael as the narrator in *Moby Dick*?" "What assumptions did the makers of American foreign policy make about the organization and strength of the Viet Cong prior to the Christmas Day bombings of 1972?" or "Can Japanese models of management be adopted by American corporations?" have no simple answers. Asking them before the beginning of a lecture gives students opportunities to offer their own hypotheses before teachers present theirs.

Questions at the beginning of a lecture serve the same function as study questions provided for assigned readings. Such questions create issues or problems for students to focus on in sorting out the information they will receive. Another value of initiating presentations with questions is that, in so doing, teachers model their own critical thinking processes and communicate to students their willingness to entertain alternatives. After such an approach, students will be less hesitant to interrupt and raise their own questions.

Teachers should note, however, that some kinds of questions do more harm than good. One of the most common approaches to generating discussion, and one of the worst, is reminiscent of the old children's game button-button-who-has-the-button. In this approach, instructors ask questions for which they have specific answers in mind. Such questions may initially produce a few raised hands, but students quickly catch on to the fact that the only real point of them is to find the "button." Answers to questions of this nature are usually factual, informational, and highly specific. They are primarily a function of recall. "How does B. F. Skinner define operant conditioning?" "Name the five steps from last week's managerial problem-solving model." Questions of this nature do little to stimulate discussion and inquiry. The questions that generate real discussion pose problems and encourage students in the formulation of judgments.

Even when teachers do their best to encourage discussion, they should not underestimate students' previous schooling in passivity and game playing. A high degree of awareness and a bit of cunning are needed to help instructors avoid the pitfalls of too much talking on their own part and too little discussion on the part of their students. Kenneth Eble suggests that "the crafty teacher will not let students be simply passive sponges, but will fool, deceive, and trick, all in the interest of getting students to question, to find out for themselves, to respond to the complexity of the world" (1983, p. 57). The crafty teacher will also know how to keep discussions on target and thus avoid the common pitfall of side-tracking, another skill of crafty students.

Once discussion has been initiated and students do venture to raise questions, the best response is to immediately bounce those questions back to the original interrogators or to other students in the class. Students know well how to get teachers to do their thinking for them, for most teachers are more than willing to demonstrate their expertise and brilliance by answering queries. However, most, if not all, student questions can be answered or at least commented insightfully upon by either the questioner or other students. Bouncing questions back to students lets them know that the teacher has confidence in their abilities, reinforces the practice of raising questions, and provides opportunities for students to develop their own critical thinking faculties.

Teachers interested in exploring discussion-leading techniques in more depth should consider the work done by the Harvard School of Business in its case studies approach to teaching. Harvard business professor C. Roland Christensen recently directed the preparation of a revised edition of *Teaching by the Case Method* (due for publication in fall 1986), which should be extremely helpful to teachers interested in incorporating more discussion into their classes. Norris Sanders's *Classroom Questions: What Kind?* (1966) offers a helpful typology of questions for use in both discussion and examinations. William Fawcett Hill's *Learning Through Discussion* (1969) is also useful.

Five Keys to Creating an Interactive Classroom

Restructuring classes so students can engage in dialogue that fosters critical thinking and reflection is a rewarding but challenging venture for teachers. The following five suggestions should make the task easier.

Begin each class with a problem or controversy. We described earlier the advantage of an opening problem or controversy for capturing student interest and encouraging discussion. Beginning a class with a problem or question related to the topic for that day also helps students settle down and focus their attention. This is a matter of no little importance.

Teachers must bear in mind that it normally takes at least five minutes for students to settle down and begin to pay attention to what is being said. Consider for a moment all the preoccupations that may be buzzing in students' heads when they enter a classroom. They may have just rushed over from another class where they were engrossed in a totally different subject. They may be passionately involved in a new romance or irritated at a friend or roommate. Adult students often come to class directly from their jobs and may not have had time to eat. Personal relationships, postpubescent sexual urges, financial worries, graduate school pressures, divorce, change in job, the homecoming dance—any concern may fill students' minds. The only safe assumption teachers can make is that most of the time (except perhaps on examination day) students' minds are initially elsewhere.

Consider beginning each class session with a brief problem-solving exercise. I have successfully used short magazine or newspaper clippings that relate to the concept I intend the class to discuss that day. The article, along with one or two key questions, is on the students' desks when they enter the classroom. I give them five minutes after the formal class starting time to read the article and answer the questions. I then have them respond to this exercise in small groups as a way of raising questions and issues and kicking off the discussion for the day. I was skeptical of this approach when a colleague first suggested it to me, but I soon learned that students not only enjoyed it but began showing up early so they could spend more time working on the short exercises. Several examples of problem-solving exercises appear in the next chapter.

Another way to raise questions or arouse interest is to open the class by commenting on something happening in the college community that relates to the topic at hand. References to movies and television shows also come in handy when they are relevant to teaching concerns. Teachers involved in research should consider sharing their work with the class if it relates to an appropriate topic or concept. Whatever technique you choose, keep in mind that the first few minutes of class time are vital in setting a tone and focusing attention on the topic for the day.

Here are a few examples showing how instructors can use articles to stimulate discussion.

- To introduce a new concept
  An economics teacher distributes a newspaper editorial on rising gasoline prices and uses it to introduce a discussion

about common misunderstandings of supply-and-demand theory.

- To reinforce previously introduced concepts
  After a lecture and discussion on Maslow's hierarchy of needs, students in an introductory psychology class are asked to clip and bring to class an advertisement from a magazine or newspaper and to explain how that ad appeals specifically to one or more of the levels of Maslow's hierarchy.

- To analyze and compare theoretical concepts
  Students in a physical anthropology class are given an article from *Time* magazine describing the discovery in Asia of an ancient humanoid skull. They are asked to comment on this article in light of previously assigned reading detailing Richard Leakey's theory about the African origins of human beings.

Use silence to encourage reflection. Problem solving, dialogue, sometimes even heated exchanges of opinion can all contribute to the development of critical thinking—but so can *silence.* Unfortunately, creative silence is noticeably missing from most college classrooms. Even teachers who feel comfortable when engaging students in discourse often feel uncomfortable with silence. This is natural, for our culture is a noisy one. We so worship words and activity that calm and silence seem either a waste of time or a threat.

Yet good teachers know that serious thinking demands periods of silence, reflection, and incubation that are uninterrupted by any words, no matter how well intended or "meaningful." Part of learning to think critically involves quiet pondering—letting things "simmer" or "cook" awhile before opening one's mouth. Students need time to mull over and digest all the new information, concepts, and methodologies being presented to them. John Dewey put it nicely when he said, "All reflection involves, at some point, stopping external observations and reactions so that an idea may mature. . . . The metaphors of digestion and assimilation, that so readily occur to mind in connection with rational elaboration, are highly instructive" ([1910] 1982, p. 210).

Some of the best times to pause for silence occur during periods of questioning. When students do not readily volunteer answers to questions, there is no need for teachers to rush in to fill the gap. Though both teachers and students initially may feel uncomfortable with silence, they can learn to relax and use it to deepen their thinking.

Even when they do choose to answer student questions, teachers can model reflection by engaging in it themselves. Rather than immediately opening their mouths, they might use a pause to show students that teachers also need time to respond thoughtfully to questions that call for judgment and reflection. Silence is probably the most underestimated of all teaching tools and also the most pregnant with possibility.

Arrange classroom space to encourage interaction. Most of us have noticed how important physical setting is to efficiency and comfort in our work. Today's corporations hire "human engineering" specialists and spend a considerable amount of time and money to make sure that the physical environments of buildings are conducive to the activities of their inhabitants.

Similarly, college classroom space should be designed to facilitate the activity of critical thinking. We may be on the verge of the twenty-first century, but step into almost any college classroom and you step back in time at least a hundred years. Desks are normally in straight rows, so students can clearly see the teacher but not all their peers. The assumption behind such an arrangement is obvious: Everything of importance comes from the teacher.

With a little imagination and effort, unless desks are bolted to the floor, the teacher can correct this situation and create space that encourages interchange among students. In small or standard-size classes, chairs, desks, and tables can be arranged in a variety of configurations: circles, rectangles, U-shapes, or semicircles. The primary goal should be for everyone to be able to see everyone else. Larger classes, particularly those held in lecture halls, unfortunately allow much less flexibility.

Arrangement of the classroom should also facilitate division of students into small groups for discussion or problem-solving exercises. Small classes with mobile desks and tables pose no problem. Even in large lecture halls, it is possible for students to turn around and form small clusters of four to six. Breaking a class into small groups provides more opportunities for students to interact with each other, think out loud, and see how other students' thinking processes operate—all essential elements in developing new modes of critical thinking.

In courses that regularly use a small group format, students might be asked to stay in the same small groups throughout the course. A colleague of mine allows students to move around during the first two weeks, until they find a group they are comfortable with. He then asks them to stay in the same seat, with the same group, from that time on. This not only creates a comfortable setting for interaction but helps him learn student names and faces. Figure 5 shows suggestions for seating arrangements in both large and small classes.

Wherever possible, extend class time. Critical thinking is best nurtured when students have adequate time to become thoroughly engaged in reflection. The traditional fifty- or sixty-minute class length used in most colleges and universities is so antithetical to serious reflective thought and so arbitrary that its persistence is truly amazing. Wherever flexibility is possible, teachers should consider meeting twice a week in ninety-minute classes, or even once a week in three-hour classes, rather than using the usual one-hour, three-times-a-week format.

In the ADAPT program at the University of Nebraska at Lincoln, classes meet in fifty-minute and seventy-five-minute formats, with three-hour labs in the sciences. Because ADAPT is a small program in a large university, it is more or less bound to a traditional short class length. ADAPT coordinator Robert Fuller acknowledges that longer classes are much better than shorter ones for teaching critical thinking skills. But success of the ADAPT program even in its limited format is proof that good things can occur in fifty-minute classes if teachers are creative.

Create a hospitable environment. Attempts to encourage discussion and interchange are basically attempts to make the

Figure 5. Ways to Reform Large Groups into Small Groups for Discussion.

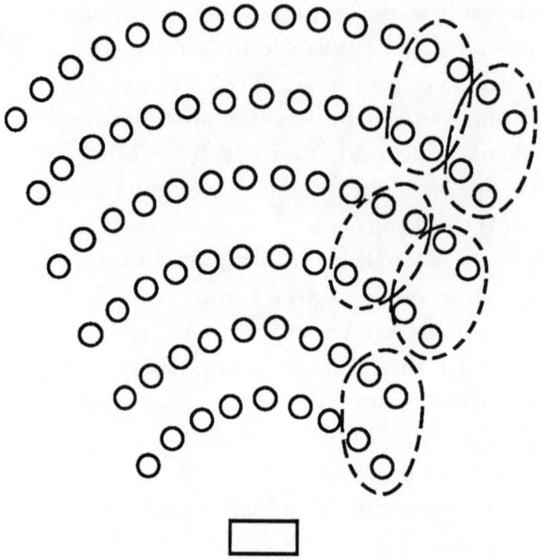

Lecture Hall

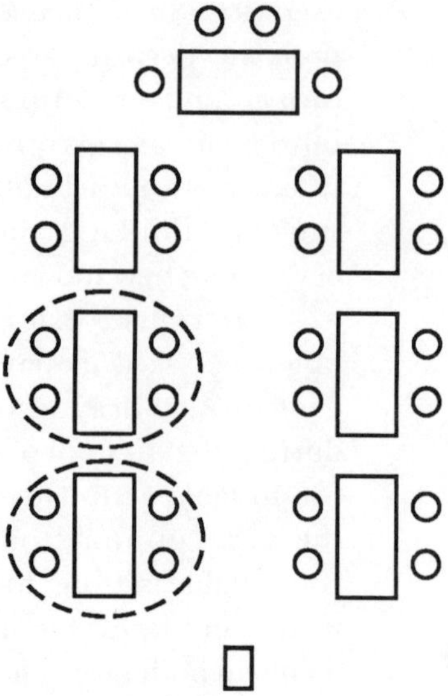

Tables in Horseshoe Arrangement

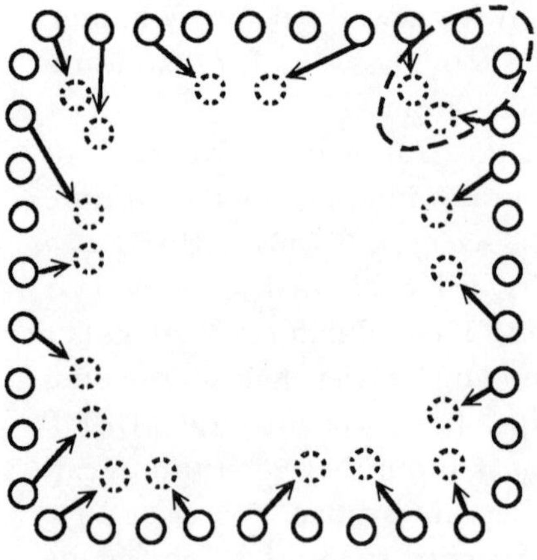

Movable Desks in Classroom

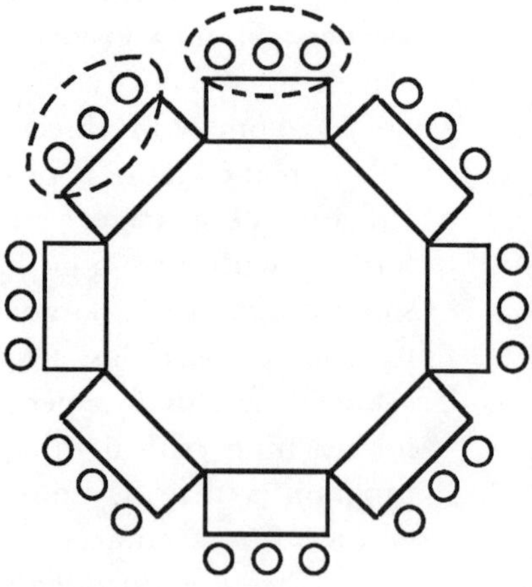

Tables in a Circle

college classroom into a more hospitable setting, a place where both students and teachers can feel safe and develop confidence. Such a setting is important for the development of critical thinking abilities. Students need the stimulus of discussion, dialogue, and debate to shake them from their old mental structures, but they also need a sense of security as they formulate and test new modes of thinking.

Feedback is essential for a teacher who is trying to work out the most supportive and fruitful class environment. A request for evaluation made around the third or fourth week of a course can often be very helpful in this regard. This request must, however, be presented as carefully formulated questions. Merely asking students "how things are going" may open the door to a gripe session or stony silence. After all, students will naturally feel some discomfort when offering evaluative comments directly to teachers.

For years I tried to initiate mini-evaluation sessions partway through my classes, with little success. Then recently I decided to break students into small groups, ask one person in each group to serve as a recorder, and have the groups brainstorm for five minutes what they needed more of or less of, along with any other suggestions they might have. The small group process lent anonymity to the proceedings, and for the first time the general tone and content of the comments became truly helpful.

Much of the success in teaching critical thinking rests with the tone that teachers set in their classrooms. Students must be led gently into the active roles of discussing, dialoguing, and problem solving. They will watch very carefully to see how respectfully teachers field comments and will quickly pick up nonverbal cues that show how open teachers really are to student questions and contributions.

One could say that the best classroom environment for critical thinking is one in which students are welcome guests and teachers hospitable hosts. In closing this chapter, I would like to quote at length from Henri Nouwen's comments on teaching in his book *Reaching Out*. Nouwen's words describe the essence of a setting where teacher and students can learn from each other as they explore new modes of critical thinking.

> The hospitable teacher has to reveal to the students that they have something to offer. Many students have been for so many years on the receiving side, and have become so deeply impregnated with the idea that there is still a lot more to learn, that they have lost confidence in themselves and can hardly imagine that they themselves have something to give. . . . Therefore, the teacher has first of all to reveal, to take away the veil covering many students' intellectual life, and help them see that their own life experiences, their own insights and convictions, their own intuitions and formulations are worth serious attention. It is so easy to impress students with books they have not read, with terms that they have not heard, with situations with which they are unfamiliar. It is much more difficult to be a receiver who can help the students to distinguish carefully between the wheat and weeds in their own lives and to show the beauty of the gifts they are carrying with them. . . . Teachers who can detach themselves from their need to impress and control, and who can allow themselves to become receptive for the news that their students carry with them, will find that it is in receptivity that gifts become visible [1966, p. 61].

6

Designing Effective Written Assignments

Creating written assignments that encourage critical thinking is a challenge because there are so few appropriate models. Most college teachers use the same kinds of assignments and examinations they experienced as students. This usually means a continued reliance on objective tests, standard essay or blue-book exams, and other methods that emphasize recall of information rather than critical thinking abilities. In the traditional repertoire of college assignments, only the term paper offers potential for demonstrating critical thinking abilities. And, for many teachers, the results of term papers are often disappointing.

By their very nature, problems and issues that require critical thinking do not lend themselves to examinations with simple correct or incorrect answers nor even necessarily to the traditional term paper format. In assessing critical thinking abilities it is often as important to know *how* a student arrived at a conclusion as it is to know the conclusion itself. Assignments in critical thinking should give students opportunities to puzzle over issues, to sort things out, and to formulate their own independent judgments. Traditional college assignments rarely provide these opportunities.

Before we discuss characteristics of effective critical thinking assignments, it is worthwhile to explore in somewhat more detail the liabilities of the term paper. Such an exploration is necessary because the term paper is so often relied upon to assess critical thinking abilities.

Reassessing the Traditional Term Paper

The shortcomings of major term papers are well known to most college teachers. Such papers consume inordinate amounts of time for both students and teachers, and the time is not well spent. Even students who exhibit good thinking abilities in classroom discussions usually produce term papers that are quite unimpressive. Term papers often prove to be merely exercises in recapitulating the thoughts of others—and often resemble sixth-grade book reports. The problem is that most students feel intimidated when asked to analyze the work of writers who clearly know more than the students do about a given subject. As a result, the students resort to summarizing and paraphrasing the "experts" rather than exercising their own judgments.

One of the major reasons for term paper assignments getting so muddled is imprecise instructions. When students are asked to "analyze" or "critique" a reading, without knowing exactly what is intended by those terms, the results are predictably disappointing. Analyze in light of what? Critique from what perspective? The word *analyze* might mean summarize, compare, contrast, take apart, reassemble, or regurgitate—in short, it will mean different things to different students. *Critique* often is translated as "criticize," causing many students to produce a mere list of personal likes and dislikes.

Even when semantic difficulties are clarified, other problems remain. A certain mindset of fear and confusion seems to accompany the assignment of a major paper. As a result, students tend to focus their attention on form rather than content. The first questions students normally ask about term paper assignments are "How many pages?" and "Do we have to use footnotes?" Thus, energy is spent trying to fill the minimum number of pages and making sure to use proper margins, punctuation, and footnotes rather than formulating a cogent argument or offering support for a well-conceived conclusion.

Given all these liabilities, why do so many teachers persevere in assigning term papers? McKeachie (1969) suggests that partial reinforcement is the culprit. Teachers receive just enough good papers to inhibit their exploring other avenues of evaluation.

On those rare occasions when term papers work, they do provide a good means of assessing thinking abilities. The problem is that rare successes do not provide a sound methodology for teaching critical thinking.

There is also, of course, the element of familiarity. Most teachers, through their own graduate and undergraduate schooling, have become accustomed to writing term papers. They seem to feel that it is their academic duty to require term papers from students—and that they are "shortchanging" their students' education if they fail in this duty.

But perhaps the primary reason term papers continue to be assigned is due to popular misconceptions about the way that critical thinking abilities develop. College teachers have long assumed that critical thinking abilities emerge only through a period of incubation, after students have digested sufficient information and have been tested in more structured ways for recall of content. According to this assumption, objective tests, quizzes, and essay exams help prepare students to develop critical thinking skills. The real linchpin in this supposed process, however, is the term, or research, paper assigned near the end of a course. This paper supposedly provides an almost irresistible medium for the expression of critical thinking abilities that have been incubating throughout the course.

If the development of critical thinking is really a mysterious internal process, the fruition of which can be assessed only at the end of ten or twelve weeks of incubation, then term papers may be as good a means as any of assessing that process. If, however, as has been argued thus far, development of critical thinking skills is more analogous to the development of motor skills, which need regular practice and exercise, then traditional term papers are ill chosen because they demand too much of students too late in the course.

Characteristics of Effective Written Assignments

The exact nature of written assignments that are effective in teaching critical thinking will vary with both the discipline and the ways the individual instructor defines and teaches critical thinking. All, however, will probably share certain basic characteristics. These include a stepwise development of critical thinking skills, a focus on real problems and issues, and clear, unambiguous instructions.

Stepwise Development of Skills. A central consideration in the design of any critical thinking assignment is the building-block nature of critical thinking processes. As we explained earlier, students do not learn to think critically merely by acquiring increasingly complex layers of discipline content, as traditional pedagogy assumes. Rather, they need to practice actively the component skills of critical thinking. They should begin with simple operations, such as summarizing, recognizing basic issues, identifying key concepts, and learning to ask appropriate questions. They can then build toward more complex and sophisticated skills, such as recognizing assumptions and creating and critiquing arguments. Learning to think critically is like developing any other skill. It must be practiced over and over again, at increasingly complex levels, before it is mastered. Assignments should be woven into the fabric of a course in an orderly and sequential manner so that, by the end of the course, students have mastered skills and attitudes that can serve as a foundation for future critical thinking endeavors.

In this regard, it is helpful to consider more and shorter assignments rather than fewer and longer ones. While designing an integrated series of short assignments initially makes more work for the teacher than do traditional tests and papers, in the long run such a series has a number of advantages. A series of short analytical papers that builds critical thinking skills is much more likely to produce desirable results than one major term paper for which students have little or no preparation. Correcting and commenting on short assignments is also much less of a burden to teachers, and more likely to get done quickly, than facing a seemingly insurmountable stack of major projects or papers.

Another advantage of short assignments is that they give immediate feedback to students. Quizzes, problem-solving exercises, and brief simulations that can be completed and discussed in class provide far more powerful learning tools than papers and exams that are returned to students weeks or months after the fact.

By making students immediately aware of the strengths and weaknesses of their responses, prompt feedback plays an essential role in the trial-and-error efforts so necessary to the development of critical thinking.

Focus on Real Problems and Issues. A second important characteristic of effective written assignments in critical thinking is that they relate to real problems and issues and draw upon students' own experiences. As we noted in Chapter Three, students must begin with the concrete before they can move on to the abstract. The problem with many traditional assignments rests with their detached, abstract nature. For example, if a philosophy teacher asked students to "discuss the relationship between Jean-Paul Sartre's concepts of anguish and freedom," such a query would likely result in a rather dispassionate clarification of terminology. Another approach is to pose a problem close to all college students' hearts. "A friend, who is a senior in college, has just broken up with his girlfriend. Your friend is in deep despair over this loss. He says he cannot bear to face the future alone. How would you explain your friend's feelings and condition in terms of Sartre's concepts of anguish and freedom?"

Students must be made to feel that they are struggling with real problems and issues, and not, in Whitehead's words, "merely executing intellectual minuets" ([1929] 1967, p. 10). Exercises that ask students to analyze problems related to their own immediate experience prevent their writing from drifting off into the ethereal realm that so often characterizes academic assignments.

Give Clear Unambiguous Instructions. A third feature of effective written assignments is that the purpose of each assignment be clearly thought out and that instructions be open to as little misinterpretation as possible. Whenever my students have uniformly bungled an assignment, the problem can always be traced to some legitimate misinterpretation of my instructions. I find it much better to err on the side of overexplicitness—"Compare the B. F. Skinner article to the fourfold model of human behavior presented in class by citing similarities and differences. Support your argument with brief quotations from the article"—than to risk misinterpretation or leave students to their own devices by simply asking them to "analyze the B. F. Skinner article in light of classroom discussions."

One of the most illuminating events in a recent series of teaching seminars I attended occurred during the final week, when teachers shared with each other examples of their written assignments and essay exams. Each participant was asked to select a written assignment that both required students to demonstrate critical thinking abilities and was characterized by clarity of instructions. Participants then presented these assignments to the group, just as they would to students. Without exception, each presentation was followed by numerous questions resulting from legitimate misinterpretations of instructions. The exercise was very instructive and helped explain why students so often miss the mark in completing written assignments and examinations. As a result of this experience, I always share drafts of my exams and written assignments with one or two colleagues and ask their candid assessment of both the intent of the assignment and the clarity of its instructions. It is safe to assume that if one's peers cannot understand an assignment, students are even more likely to be confused.

Five Types of Written Assignments for Critical Thinking

The sections that follow will describe and present models for five types of written assignments that have been found effective in developing critical thinking skills. In line with the criteria described in the last section, all are short assignments that sequentially build critical thinking skills, draw on real problems, and provide clear, unambiguous instructions. Naturally, readers are welcome to adapt, modify, and reconstruct these models as they develop their own critical thinking assignments.

Most of the assignments were created by the faculty of Metropolitan State University. Because the programs at Metro U focus on business, human services, communications, and the humanities, the physical and natural sciences are underrepresented in our samples. Interested science teachers are referred to the work of Robert Karplus and others who have created model exercises for the development of critical thinking in the sciences (see Karplus and others, 1978).

Brief Summaries. Before students can realistically be expected to critique or analyze material in any discipline, they need to develop more basic thinking skills, such as those involved in identifying central concepts and issues and summarizing these from readings and related materials. Many teachers underestimate the critical and analytical skills involved in simple exercises like summarizing. Summarizing new materials does not mean simply condensing or paraphrasing them. It involves processing concepts and issues in terms of one's own experience and understanding. The ability to summarize also involves the skill of prioritizing.

For students new to a discipline, summarizing discipline-related materials is like sorting through a pile of rocks, looking for unpolished agates. Unless one has some idea of what an agate looks like, the task can be frustrating and even hopeless. Summarizing requires sorting through words and ideas, trying to separate the essential from the nonessential. Learning to master the basic terms, concepts, and issues of an unfamiliar discipline is not easy, particularly when students are studying other unfamiliar disciplines at the same time. Instructors therefore should give priority to initial assignments that highlight essential concepts, issues, and principles and require students to translate these into their own words and experience.

Methodologically speaking, summaries are great tools for teaching critical thinking, because they help students fix ideas in their minds, provide practice in identifying main issues and concepts, and offer opportunities for prioritizing information (Corner, 1983). Summaries function much like study questions in helping students focus attention on specific concepts and issues. Written summaries also give teachers important clues about the success of their teaching endeavors. If student summaries of lectures uniformly miss certain main points, there is likely to be a defect in the teacher's presentations. A final benefit of brief summaries is they can be quickly commented on and returned to students, thus providing feedback on students' understanding of basic concepts and issues.

The following are typical subjects for which written summaries may be usefully assigned. A specific example of an assignment is given for each.

- A chapter in a book or assigned reading:
  "In two brief paragraphs summarize Chapter 6 in the abnormal psychology text. Focus on the concept of alienation and give an example from your own experience."
- A lecture or classroom presentation:
  "What were the main points of today's lecture? Summarize those points briefly in your own words."
- A period of classroom discussion:
  "Today's classroom discussion covered a lot of different ideas. What points were most helpful to you in understanding the concept of artistic perspective?"
- A film or videotape shown in class:
  "Hopefully, today's film helped to clarify the concept of marginal profit. Imagine for a minute that you had to summarize this film for a twelve-year-old child. What would you tell that child?"

Short Analytical Papers. We have already described several reasons why short analytical papers offer an improvement over major term papers. One of the primary values of short assignments is that they can be used as building blocks to teach the constituent skills of a larger critical thinking process. The following series of four paper assignments from a course in American history offers a good example of this teaching method. Though the four assignments, taken individually, differ little from typical written college assignments, it can be seen when they are considered together that the teacher has taken pains to build basic skills of critical thinking in his progression. By the time the fourth paper is assigned, students are well prepared to complete this complex assignment because they have practiced the necessary constituent skills in the three previous assignments.

One of the main strategies in the course, called "Empire in Conflict," is to review key events and historical documents in America between 1750 and the early 1900s, with a focus on American expansionism. Themes include the historical sources of American expansionism, American political economy and ideology, and conflicts between the development of an empire and the demands of a balanced representative government and individual liberties. The four short analytical assignments developed for this course are shown in Exhibits 3 through 6.

Problem-Solving Exercises Using Popular Media. One of the more challenging aspects of teaching critical thinking is helping students comprehend and appropriate abstract concepts and principles. Whenever teachers build bridges between concrete, everyday ideas and more abstract, academic concepts, they are

Exhibit 3. "Empire in Conflict": Written Assignment 1.

You are to read James Madison's *Federalist No. 10.* This is a difficult essay, so you'll need to read it more than once.

For the first part of this assignment, write two pages that describe the main points Madison is trying to communicate to his readers. In other words, boil this document down to its major points and line of argument. Summarize these in your own words, *without* using direct quotes or extensive paraphrasing.

For the second part of the assignment, step into the shoes of a historian and speculate on the value of this document for understanding some of the main themes of expansionism we discussed the first night of class. Take one or two pages to discuss the ways in which Madison's ideas reflect the themes we outlined in class.

The two sections of your paper should not exceed five pages of typed, double-spaced copy.

Tasks involved in this assignment:

- summarizing a document in the student's own words
- recognizing concepts and themes presented in class
- speculating on the impact Madison had on American expansionism

Exhibit 4. "Empire in Conflict": Written Assignment 2.

This assignment asks you to address the same tasks of historical inquiry you practiced in Assignment 1—recognizing and summarizing main points. However, in this assignment you will also be asked to analyze and compare historical documents by citing some of their similarities and differences.

Background Information: Near the end of the war with Mexico, Senator Sidney Breese of Illinois urged the annexation of all Mexico. Breese, a Democrat, represented a growing movement that included support from Whigs, Jacksonian Democrats, Southern and Northern expansionists, and slavery and commercial interests. His expansionism foreshadows other movements of the next few years that were aimed at Central America and the Caribbean.

Read Breese's speech before the U.S. Senate; then prepare a four- to six-page paper that includes the following:

1. A one- to two-page summary, in your own words, of what Senator Breese is proposing and the arguments he sets forth in favor of his proposal.
2. Two pages in which you compare Breese's views with those expressed in the excerpt from John Quincy Adams's *Diary,* focusing on subjects and issues that concern both men (for example, the extent of the American union).
3. One page in which you reflect on why *one* of the following early exponents of American empire—Madison, Adams, Clay, or Monroe—would have probably opposed Breese's appeal at this point in American history.

Tasks involved in this assignment:

- summarizing in the student's own words
- comprehending new issues in the debate on expansionism
- recognizing similarities and differences between writers
- reflecting on implications of source documents

fostering critical thinking. Problem-solving exercises built around newspaper and magazine articles are one of the most creative and productive forms of such bridge building.

Because newspapers, magazines, and other forms of printed media are written for mass audiences, they avoid the pitfalls of academic jargon. Thus, they provide a variety of excellent opportunities for drawing analogies and relating everyday

Exhibit 5. "Empire in Conflict": Written Assignment 3.

This assignment asks you to examine some conflicting interpretations of American foreign policy in the late nineteenth and early twentieth centuries, as seen through the eyes of three different historians.

Read carefully the following articles:

Walter LeFeber, "Preserving the American System"
William A. Williams, "The Open Door Policy"
Robert Beisner, "Limits to the Economic Interpretation"

Then write a paper, not to exceed six typed, double-spaced pages, that fulfills the following assignments.

1. In the first two pages of your paper, summarize in your own words the main points in the LeFeber and Williams articles.
2. In an additional one-page section, argue for or against the following proposition: that the LeFeber and Williams articles can be joined together into a common outlook on the period between 1880 and 1908. Do the interpretations of the two historians complement one another and follow a similar line of reasoning? Explain how they do or do not. Use brief quotes to support your argument.
3. In a final two-page section, briefly summarize Beisner's major points and evaluate one of these points by either defending or criticizing that point in light of lectures, discussions, previous readings, and the Williams and LeFeber articles.

Tasks involved in this assignment:

- summarizing main points in an argument
- developing an argument and supporting it
- relating ideas in one reading to those in other sources of information

experience to more abstract concepts studied in the classroom. As Chapter Five noted, short articles can be distributed for reading at the beginning of a class and used as a point of departure for classroom discussion or small group discussion. They can also be used in effective written assignments.

Another important value of assignments based on printed media is the challenge they present to students' habitual ways of thinking. Students often labor under the misapprehension that

Exhibit 6. "Empire in Conflict": Written Assignment 4.

Recently, President Reagan appointed a National Bipartisan Commission on Central America to provide advice on appropriate elements of a "long-term United States policy that will best respond to the challenges of social, economic, and democratic development in that region, and to internal and external threats to its security and stability."

No one appointed to the commission qualified as an historian, let alone an historian of American diplomatic policy, nor did any prominent historians of diplomatic policy testify before the commission. Accordingly, the commission's historical background section is sparse and says little about what relationship American diplomatic history and foreign policy concepts have to Central America's development and history.

For your final written assignment, which should be a maximum of eight typed, double-spaced pages, do the following:

1. In an introductory section of two pages, make a case for or against the inclusion of an historian on the President's Bipartisan Commission. Make certain to outline a convincing argument and offer evidence for your point of view. (I will not be offended if you make a case against including an historian.)
2. Imagine yourself to be an American diplomatic historian. In three to five pages, write a position paper to be submitted to the President as an addendum to the commission's report. Alert the President to basic issues, concepts, events, themes, and interpretations of American diplomatic history that you think are critical to decision making on Central American policy. Limit yourself to a *few* major points in order to make an effective presentation that uses what you have studied, discussed, and listened to in this class. (In other words, *do not* present a long list of issues that contain no analysis or explanation.) Use references and footnotes when appropriate.

Tasks involved in this assignment:

- practical application of historical theory to a matter of contemporary U.S. policy
- use of skills in summarizing, comparing, evaluating sources, and making a cogent argument

---

everything appearing in print—especially in supposedly "objective" news reporting—is true. Exercises that force students to raise questions regarding point of view, opinion, or bias in the popular press can help to dispel this illusion and assist students in developing a healthy skepticism about the printed word.

Newspaper editorials, which more openly reflect opinion, also provide lively opportunities for teaching some of the attitudinal aspects of critical thinking. Students usually enjoy analyzing and discussing the thoughts of such eminent columnists as William Buckley, Ellen Goodman, and Russell Baker. Attitudes of reflection and skepticism are an important part of critical thinking, and exercises that ask students to look for assumptions and to critique arguments help instill these attitudes.

Teachers can easily adapt print media to develop written exercises for use in teaching and evaluating students' critical thinking abilities. Articles should be brief enough to be read in five minutes. As was suggested earlier, it is best to begin exercises at a fairly low level of critical thinking, teaching students to summarize, recognize main points, and draw analogies to abstract concepts and principles. In addition to their teaching and evaluative purposes, brief written exercises can be used at the beginning of a class period to settle students down and focus their attention. A brief written exercise at the start of each class can help students center in on the task for that class period and provides a convenient opportunity for students to disengage from previous preoccupations. Two examples of print media problem-solving exercises are shown in Exhibits 7 and 8.

Outside Projects. Another way to help students apply classroom theory to practical experience is to assign short projects to be done outside of class. Such exercises provide students with opportunities to think about and evaluate their own concrete experiences. The assignments should be brief enough to be completed between class sessions and should require a minimum of special props and equipment. Simple projects of observation or interview that draw on students' life experiences and resources work best.

One pitfall in designing exercises of this nature is leaving them too open-ended. Teachers need to be clear regarding the exact purpose and nature of each exercise. What specific concepts, principles, or issues are being developed? Are students adequately prepared to complete the exercise? Are instructions clear, or might they be open to misinterpretation?

To ensure desired outcomes, it is best to provide a structured format for outside exercises. Written instructions give students

Exhibit 7. "Literature of Existentialism": Problem Solving.

Read the attached newspaper article on loneliness.

Objective Reporting

According to Professor Weiss, what is the cause of social and emotional loneliness?

What does he suggest is the cure?

Identifying Assumptions

Do you think Professor Weiss feels loneliness is good or bad? Give a brief quotation to support your answer.

The last two paragraphs are particularly interesting. What do you think are the assumptions behind these closing remarks?

Related Concepts

Last week we discussed the theme of forlornness in the writings of Jean-Paul Sartre. How would Sartre agree or disagree with Dr. Weiss on the cause of loneliness?

Exhibit 8. "Introduction to Economics": Problem Solving.

Read the attached editorial responding to David Stockman's analysis of "the farm problem."

1. Summarize in your own words the main points of the writer's argument.

2. How does the writer's interpretation of "the farm problem" compare with the economic model of "perfect competition" we are discussing in class?

3. Do you think higher food prices are the inevitable result of "an oligopolistic system of food production"?

---

something to have in hand while they are engaged in the activity. Since exercises of this nature can be entertaining as well as educational, students may be carried away by unbridled enthusiasm unless they have a structured format to follow. Exhibits 9 and 10 show two examples of outside projects.

Simulations. A weakness of many college writing assignments is the lack of a "real world" context. Robert Gremore offers some valuable insights on why a realistic context is so important to the success of any writing endeavor.

> In the everyday world, writers almost always write about a *particular topic,* for a *particular audience,* to accomplish a *particular purpose.* Those three things add up to a "rhetorical situation." In everyday life, rhetorical situations are the givens within which a writer works. Generally, writers know what sort of problem a given piece of writing is supposed to solve and they know the characteristics of the audience for whom they are writing. Those two kinds of knowledge help them not only to select and narrow a topic, but also to organize and draft their report. Rhetorical situations are thus great aids to a writer, guiding the way he or she selects, organizes, and presents data. . . . Unaccustomed to thinking about rhetorical situations, teachers often design writing assignments that lack them. This can be disastrous for students, who are thus deprived of crucial background information that helps real life writers decide what to write about and how to write [Gremore, 1983].

Lacking a clear rhetorical situation, students are left to their own devices in trying to decide just what the teacher, as audience, wants. Writing for a teacher as one's audience leads naturally to attempts at "psyching out" the teacher. Psyching out the teacher is not merely undergraduate gamesmanship but a mechanism for coping with "unreal" academic assignments. The more a critical thinking assignment simulates a realistic situation—that is, creates

Exhibit 9. "Sex Variation in Language": Outside Assignment.

As a follow-up to our recent reading and discussion on interruption behavior of men and women, please complete this exercise and bring it with you to our next class.

Observe a lengthy conversation (one that lasts at least ten minutes) that involves members of both sexes. As you observe (as inconspicuously as possible), focus on interruptions, taking note of (a) who interrupts whom, (b) who interrupts most, (c) who is interrupted most.

Use this format to record your results (you may need additional pages):

	Talker	Sex	Age	Status and/or occupation	Number of interruptions made	Number of times interrupted
1						
2						
3						
4						

After recording this information, think about the conversation and complete the following tasks:

1. In one paragraph, describe any connections you may have noticed between status or occupation and interruptions.
2. In one or two paragraphs, explain whether sex seems to be related to interrupting. If so, how?
3. Might there be other variables that account for the interruptions in this particular conversation? If so, what do you think they are?
4. How do your findings relate to our earlier discussion of sex roles in our culture?

Source: Adapted from Eakins and Eakins, 1978.

Exhibit 10. "Art Appreciation": Special Assignment.

At the student union this week, there is an exhibit of paintings by local artist Marie DuBonnet. Go to the exhibit before our next class and complete this exercise. Turn it in at the next class.

Choose *one* of the following paintings to analyze: "Winter Dawn," "Ghosts of the Prairie," or "Still Life." Spend at least ten minutes (it will seem like a very long time) simply observing the painting before committing any thoughts to writing. Try not to formulate any specific interpretations. Then, when you have completed your observations, answer the following questions.

1. Is the artist trying to convey a special mood or tone in this work, or are these not important aspects for analysis? Support your argument with specific observations.
2. Last week we discussed the importance of perspective in the development of any work of art. How does DuBonnet use perspective in the painting you selected?

Please complete this exercise in two to three handwritten pages. Be sure to indicate which painting you selected and number your responses to match the questions.

a real problem that demands a solution—the less time students are likely to spend worrying about what they think the teacher wants.

Gremore's remarks about rhetorical situations relate directly to recent attempts by teachers to incorporate simulation exercises into their teaching strategies. Posing a realistic problem situation, such as a counseling interview, a marketing dilemma, or the investigation of an historical artifact, helps specify topic, purpose, and audience—what Gremore defines as the basic components of a rhetorical situation. Simulations normally require students to assume a role in the problem situation and to present their analysis or findings to a particular audience. The second part of the final paper assignment in the American history class (Exhibit 6) offers a good example. In that assignment, students are asked to assume the role of a diplomatic historian and to write a position paper (purpose) on basic issues, concepts, events, and themes of American diplomatic history (topic) that will help the President (audience) make better decisions regarding U.S. involvement in Central America.

Most disciplines lend themselves to the creation of simulations. The more realistic the simulated situation, the more students are forced to grapple with real problems and freed from the abstraction that they often suppose characterizes academic writing. Though simulations work at any point in a course, they are particularly suited to final exams or projects. They can help students pull together the many threads of knowledge and new critical skills that have been developing throughout the course. Exhibits 11 and 12 show two examples of simulations.

Evaluating Written Assignments

Cognitive scientists do not understand the intricate relationship between the physical act of putting words on paper and retention, processing, and future learning. Nevertheless, common sense and years of experience tell us that for most students, writing offers one of the best means of processing, consolidating, and internalizing new knowledge. In "Writing as a Mode of Learning," Janet Emig writes, "If the most efficacious learning occurs when learning is reinforced, then writing—through its inherent reinforcing cycle involving hand, eye, and brain—marks a uniquely powerful multirepresentational mode for learning" (1977, pp. 124-125). Writing is a unique form of feedback in that it makes the product of thought *visible*. Emig argues that the importance of writing "for immediate, literal (that is, visual) rescanning and review cannot perhaps be overstated" (p. 125).

Written assignments are equally valuable to the instructor because they reveal, at least in part, what student thinking processes are like. Though it is a time-consuming process, sitting down with students to go over papers allows teachers to help the students see more explicitly their own thought processes and thus become more aware of their progress in developing new modes of critical thinking.

Of course, large class size often prohibits teachers from engaging in individual consultations with students. In that case, meaningful written comments will have to suffice. The key here is

Exhibit 11. "Marketing Research": Final Exam.

Congratulations! You have just been appointed director of marketing research, at a salary of $35,000, for a U.S. corporation with $50,000,000 in domestic sales. The company's main product line is (choose one from below). This is a new function with the company, which, until last year, was family owned. The marketing vice president has asked for a comprehensive benchmark study on the present marketing environment of the company. You are to submit a detailed research proposal that will clearly spell out all the items below. Your report is not to exceed fifteen typed pages. The recommended number of pages for each section is shown in parentheses.

1. Definition of probable data needs of marketing management (4)
2. Sources of the data (new research, secondary sources (1)
3. Design for proposed research (1)
4. Design of the sample (1)
5. Data collection devices (proposed questions, topics) (3)
6. Methods of collecting data (1)
7. Proposed methods of analysis, including statistical tests when needed (1)
8. Report outline by topic and table headings (using the format we developed in class (3)

* * * * * * * * * * * * * * *

Product	*Name*
Financial services	*I.D.S. American Express*
Snack foods	*Frito-Lay*
Fire fighting equipment	*American-La France*
Hospital disposables	*Beckton Dickenson*
Magazines	*Hitchcock*
Farm chemicals	*Giegy*
Spray painting equipment	*Graco*
Toys	*Tonka*
Coal mining equipment	*Joy*
Recreation	*Disney World*
Mail order	*Fingerhut*
Gourmet food stores	*Barbareo's*
T.V. station	*WCCO-TV*

Exhibit 12. "Nurse as Communicator": Midterm Simulation.

Simulated interview with a depressed patient:

Prior to the interview, review your notes from the past four weeks of lecture and discussion on interpersonal communication skills. Also review the resource handouts and assigned readings on depression, withdrawal, anger, and confusion. Familiarize yourself with the four situational profiles distributed at the last class. Your interview will be with one of these four patients. [Only one of the four patients is described in this model.]

The interview will take ten minutes and will be videotaped. The only people present will be you, the "client," and the instructor. After being told which of the four simulated situations you will encounter, you will have a few minutes to prepare for the interview. After the interview is completed, you will be given ten minutes of feedback from the instructor via the rating form handed out in class last week. As a final stage of the process, you will turn in next week a one-page summary of how you perceived your strengths and weaknesses in interpersonal communications in this exercise. The videotape will be available for your viewing while you prepare this response.

* * * * * * * * * * * * * *

Patient's name: Sarah Polinski   Age: 19   Diagnosis: Depression

Situation: Sarah came to the crisis center at Hennepin County Medical Center at 1:00 A.M. on May 5. She is a student at the University of Minnesota and lives in an efficiency apartment close to the university. She was here once before, at age seventeen, when a boyfriend deserted her and told her to "drop dead." At that time, she had superficial razor cuts to the wrist. She came in tonight because (1) she hasn't slept for two weeks; (2) when she tries to eat food, it "gets stuck in my throat"; (3) she cannot get her school work done because "I can't concentrate. I had a paper due in anthropology and couldn't get around to doing it." You are the staff nurse at the crisis center, working the 11:30 P.M. to 7:30 A.M. shift. You have seen the report on Sarah's visit two years ago.

---

meaningful comments. Even the best-designed assignment loses much of its force as a teaching tool when the teacher uses cryptic comments and notations in evaluating it. My memory is still alive with my own undergraduate exams and papers, the margins of which were covered with bright red checks. To this day I am not sure whether those checks indicated that I had written something insightful or had missed the point altogether.

Useful written feedback can take many forms. Some teachers write short comments in the margins of pages, while others prefer longer summations at the end of the assignment. One teacher may design rating forms or structured response sheets to be used for all students, while another may take time for consultation with each individual student.

Whatever means is chosen, students greatly appreciate clear feedback, for it forms the basis for the reality testing they need to create new structures for critical thinking.

Provision of such feedback also proves worth the time and effort for many teachers, who gain the rewards of seeing their students make major improvements in critical thinking abilities, of reading student assignments of high quality, and of helping students understand the strengths and weaknesses of their present thought processes.

7

Sharing, Challenging, Supporting: The Personal Side of Teaching Critical Thinking

An underlying theme of this book that now demands more careful consideration is the personal nature of critical thinking processes. We have stressed the importance of teachers' identifying their own frameworks for problem solving and analysis and sharing those perspectives with students. How teachers make sense of their disciplines, the issues and problems they choose to focus on, and the questions they use to address these concerns are all intimately related to personal values, interests, and commitments.

Similarly, as teachers help students adopt new modes of thinking, they need to appreciate how personal an undertaking this is for students. Developing new structures of thought requires a reassessment of students' personal values and beliefs. Teachers need to help students recognize and integrate these subjective aspects of critical thinking, neither shutting these elements out in a misguided quest for "objectivity" nor allowing thought to be unquestioningly dominated by them.

The Tension Between Subjectivity and Objectivity

It is important to stress the role of subjective elements in critical thinking because the term *critical thinking* is usually identified with a strictly impersonal or objective mode of analysis. Many people lump together the terms *objective, critical,* and *cognitive* when talking about the development of thinking processes. In so doing, they implicitly discredit *subjective, personal,* and *affective* aspects of thinking. Such a perspective seems ill informed. The force that stimulates and sustains critical thinking is often rooted in personal values and commitments, as well as a need to order one's experience rationally. Nevertheless, subjectivity and objectivity are usually perceived as mutually exclusive, and differentially valued, ways of knowing. For example, Webster's *Ninth New Collegiate Dictionary* defines *objective* as "expressing or dealing with facts or conditions as perceived without distortion by personal feelings" (1983, p. 814). *Subjectivity,* on the other hand, is identified with personal feelings and more emotionally informed modes of knowing.

In *Personal Knowledge* (1962), philosopher and chemist Michael Polanyi disputes this conventional distinction between subjective and objective modes of knowledge. Polanyi is concerned with our culture's belief that science and technology are sources of objectively verifiable truth. He challenges our worship of objective, impersonal knowledge, not by arguing for an inversion of things—that is, valuing subjectivity over objectivity—but by demonstrating the inseparability of both elements in any act of knowing.

Polanyi believes that most scientific knowledge is the result not of an impersonal, dispassionate search for truth but, rather, of scientists' passionate, personal desire to comprehend nature and find order in the universe. He agrees with cognitive scientists and developmental theorists that the desire to create order and make sense of our surroundings is one of the most basic human needs (p. 98). Polanyi's emphasis on passion and beauty as constituent elements in knowing reflects the sentiments of scientists like Carl Sagan and Lewis Thomas, who argue that subjective elements like curiosity and wonder are primary motivations for all learning. Polanyi demonstrates both that totally impersonal and objective approaches are impossible and that scientific hypotheses and theories have a subjective beauty and aesthetic all their own—a symmetry and order often independent of the "facts" involved (p. 64).

Describing scientific theories and natural laws as productions of "human artifice," Polanyi offers a dramatic example from crystallography (p. 36). Theoreticians in this field predict the shape of different chemical crystals on the basis of perfectly straight geometric planes and precise angles of intersection. The fact that many natural crystals fail to exhibit these geometrically exact patterns is of little concern to them. Any departure from the ideal is seen as a shortcoming of the crystal, not the theory (p. 42).

Polanyi is not suggesting that there are no real natural laws or that all scientific theories are so approximate in their descriptions of the physical world. He is simply saying that our human striving for ideal forms of order often outreaches what we actually perceive in nature. "Personal knowledge in science . . . claims to establish contact with reality far beyond the clues on which it relies. It commits us, passionately far beyond our comprehension, to a vision of reality" (p. 64).

Polanyi's description of personal knowledge and his challenge to the traditional distinction between subjective and objective knowledge are very germane to the teaching of critical thinking, for in raising questions about the scientific tradition of impersonal and objective knowledge, Polanyi also raises questions about the tradition of objectivity in college teaching. If Polyani is correct that interest, passion, and personal values play a crucial role in development of the theoretical foundations of the physical sciences (and they play, perhaps, an even bigger role in the social sciences and humanities), then it seems logical that these same elements should be involved in the teaching of those foundations.

Polanyi's main argument is that none of us, whether scientist or teacher, can be relieved of "the personal responsibility for our beliefs" by hiding behind the cloak of "objectifiably verifiable criteria of validity" (p. 268). It is also well nigh impossible to engage students' interest and to foster critical inquiry when subject matter is presented as frozen, objective "truth." In teaching students the knowledge base of any academic discipline, and even more in teaching them to think critically about that knowledge, instructors are really teaching frameworks or modes of perception, not mere facts and formulas. Modes of perception and interpretation, by definition, involve personal and subjective elements. As Polanyi suggests, these elements are not accidental but rather are essential to the task of critical appraisal.

Personal Aspects of Teaching

Teachers can no more teach "objectively" than scientists can pursue their research devoid of personal values and interests. Commenting on the futility of traditional advice that college teachers strive to teach objectively, Kenneth Eble suggests, "Such guidance is worse than none, and hypocritical beside, for the assertion itself arises out of values of a very different kind. Better to begin confronting the complexities of the question by acknowledging the simple truth that there is no way teachers can avoid declaring values short of denying their existence as people" (1983, p. 32).

Consciously introducing personal and subjective elements into teaching frees teachers to adopt a more human and humane style of teaching critical thinking. However, such an approach involves certain risks and tensions. For one thing, introduction of personal elements cannot be allowed to degenerate into mere capriciousness. Students will not learn to think critically simply by observing teachers trot out their personal biases, opinions, and interests. While allowing more personal and subjective elements to inform their teaching, teachers must retain a healthy dose of objectivity. This advice is not contradictory. As professional educators, teachers have an obligation to represent the theoretical foundations and assumptions of their disciplines clearly and in a relatively unbiased and objective manner.

Teachers should present both their own opinions and those of others—and, most important of all, they should distinguish clearly between the two. Students need to be very aware of this distinction, for the tension between differing perceptions and modes of thinking produces the disequilibrium so valuable in challenging their present values and thought structures and helping them develop new modes of thinking. Indeed, it is often this very tension, along with instructors' personal interests and passions, that brings disciplines to life for students. Also, paradoxically, the more openly teachers acknowledge subjective elements in their teaching, the more truly objective they show themselves to be.

Some teachers fear sharing their perceptions, values, and beliefs with students because they think they may inadvertently brainwash these young minds and convert them to their own visions of reality. Such fears are almost always unjustified. Most students have already been exposed to a wealth of values, beliefs, and perceptions from parents, peers, and previous teachers. Normally they can sift through what is presented to them, adopting some things and discarding others as they formulate, with guidance, their own methods of critical thinking.

Other teachers may fear the increase in their own vulnerability that comes from allowing teaching to become more personal. It is much easier to lecture from the pedestal of the "objective" expert. As teachers drop the defenses of detachment and authority, students become more likely to challenge their pronouncements. This can be threatening to teachers who see "rightness" as the primary sign of competence. But when teachers come to regard encouraging reflection and pressing for informed judgments as important goals, they will welcome questions and challenges as signs that students are beginning to think on their own.

Teachers can help students appreciate the personal nature of critical thinking by sharing some of their own research, focusing on problems they have had to confront. Students find it comforting to know that teachers also struggle to understand certain issues and to keep subjective and objective elements in balance. By examining openly problems they themselves find difficult to solve, or by simply highlighting generally problematical issues, teachers are, in effect, saying, "I, too, struggle to make sense of things"—an acknowledgment that students seldom hear in the classroom.

In *Physics as Metaphor,* Roger Jones offers advice to science teachers that might well be heeded by any teacher who hopes to encourage attitudes of critical inquiry. "However embarrassing and unfamiliar it is, scientists should occasionally reveal the very human process of creation which they and other scientists go through, if students are ever to believe that scientific theories are made by real people with irrational and ridiculous thoughts, rather than by logical automatons with no human weakness and temptations" (1983, p. 212).

Another method for highlighting the personal nature of critical thinking is to encourage students to raise questions about the authority of their readings and texts. Printed words in general, and textbooks and assigned readings in particular, hold a special aura of impersonal truth for many students—"if it's in the text, it must be true." They need to know that even acknowledged experts struggle to maintain a balance between subjective and objective elements in their thinking. By helping students identify instances in which an author's values and beliefs influence his or her arguments and solutions, teachers can lead students to appreciate the relative nature of much knowledge, which they otherwise perceive as absolute.

By subjecting their own conclusions to student inquiry and by raising questions about the relative nature of printed "truth," teachers model the attitudes of reflective thought. If student challenges occasionally prove viable, so that teachers find themselves readjusting their previous conclusions and developing new insights, so much the better, for humility and a willingness to reconsider conclusions are also attitudes vital to critical thinking. Students need to know that a variety of respected opinions exist on any topic and that their teachers, texts, and readings are not the final repositories of truth. Indeed, only by moving away from simplistic conceptions of "truth" can students develop into critical thinkers.

Personal Aspects of Learning

While teachers often err on the side of trying to eliminate subjectivity from their teaching, students usually benefit from holding subjective elements in abeyance. As we noted in Chapter Three, a primary task of the teacher of critical thinking is helping students move beyond limited, egocentric modes of thought. Piaget says that the child "is egocentric through ignorance of his own subjectivity" (1976, p. 160). Piaget perhaps underestimated the tenacity of this subjectivity: Many college students still possess it.

Developmental theorists such as William Perry (1970), Lawrence Kohlberg (1969), and Carol Gilligan (1982) agree that one of the major blocks to development of critical thinking abilities is the extremely personal nature of thought processes. The work of these three individuals has adapted and expanded Piaget's learning theory (which focused on logical, rational, and objective elements) by discussing moral and ethical aspects of thought processes.

These theorists' view of personal beliefs as barriers to critical thought makes good sense. If our thought structures are the ways in which we organize our perceptions to make sense of the world, it seems natural that we would have a strong vested interest in maintaining those structures. Once I have made sense of the world, or even a small part of it, I will not react kindly to people who criticize, let alone try to rearrange, the result. Teachers thus need to take very seriously the difficulty of moving a student from one thought structure to another.

By focusing on the transitions between learning stages, or what he prefers to call "positions," William Perry provides helpful insights into this process. Perry is fascinated by the drama of cognitive and ethical development—the transition from one position (stage) to another—and the "ingenuity of the ways students found to move from a familiar pattern of meanings that had failed them to a new vision that promised to make sense of their broadening experience, while it also threatened them with unanticipated implications for their selfhood and their lives" (1981, p. 78). Perry's comment reiterates the point that a great deal is at stake here. Development of critical thinking skills is not a dispassionate learning process, in which students need only be shown a new way of perceiving things in order to follow it, but a threatening encounter that challenges one's very "selfhood."

Perry formulates his own schema of development to explain how the movement from a simplistic egocentric universe to a more complex social world view takes place. Though he seldom uses the term *critical thinking,* his schema clearly reflects a progression of critical thinking abilities. Perry posits nine developmental positions, but for purposes of our discussion, we will synthesize them to four primary positions.

The first position can be called *dualism.* This is a position of "cognitive simplicity," in which students believe that the world is divided into the *right and good* versus the *wrong and bad* (Perry,

p. 79). Teachers are viewed as authority figures who know this distinction and communicate it to students. If students disagree with their teachers' interpretations, it is because they recognize another source of authority, perhaps family or peers.

In the next major position, *multiplicity*, students come to realize that uncertainty exists regarding solutions to problems and issues and that authorities don't always have clear answers. Students at this stage still believe, or at least hope, that there really are "right" answers but the authorities just have not discovered them yet. In areas where right answers are not known, diversity of opinions and values is seen as legitimate and tolerable (p. 79).

In Perry's third major position, *relativism*, complexity increases. In this position, students admit that there are areas in which many points of view exist and that the context of a problem helps to determine its possible solutions (p. 80). There is an important shift here from focusing on an external source of judgment to developing one's own mode of thinking. "Authorities" no longer determine how the students think; instead, students begin to acknowledge making their own decisions.

Perry's final position is called *commitment*. In the face of growing relativism and complexity, students consciously choose values and accept responsibility for their choices (p. 80).

We cannot cite any one of these positions as the point at which critical thinking begins. Most college teachers would consider it a major advance in some students' critical thinking processes to move from a position of dualism to one of multiplicity. The real value in Perry's work is the insight it offers into the reasons why most students *do not* think critically. We will focus on just one example of a transition, that from dualism to multiplicity, as a way of appreciating the personal struggle involved in adopting a more critical mode of thinking.

One of my colleagues teaches an introductory social science course in which she asks students to look at differing assumptions that social scientists make about human behavior. In one of the first classes, she considers human behavior from the perspective of animal behavior, focusing on questions of aggression and territoriality. Part of her presentation touches briefly on evolutionary theory. A few years ago, just after this session on animal behavior, a student confronted this teacher and complained bitterly that she was teaching evolution, which went against his personal religious beliefs. He said he was therefore dropping the class. The teacher tried to discuss her position, explaining that comparison with animals was only one of the perspectives she would be exploring; and she urged the student to stay and consider some of the others. He respectfully declined, however, saying that he did not want to entertain any discussion of evolution.

This student's position on evolution was a dualistic one: Evolutionary theory was wrong, and his own beliefs were correct. It is not, however, the student's strong commitment to his own values that characterizes his thinking as dualistic, but his refusal to entertain other viewpoints. It is the *rigidity* of his position—his blindness to his own subjectivity. Even entertaining the possibility of another view of human behavior was apparently a very risky and threatening undertaking for him, causing him to experience a painful confrontation between the personal values embedded in his own view of human behavior and a conflicting set of values and assumptions.

What is particularly interesting about this case is that the student in question was known for doing excellent work in his major area of study, accounting. When confronted with figures and a balance sheet, he exhibited fine critical thinking skills. In the area of accounting, then, this student may have been highly developed in terms of Perry's positions. But in areas related to his religious belief system, he was clearly stuck at what Perry would call a dualistic position. Moving him from that position probably would have required a major and very sensitive effort.

All personal barriers to critical thinking are not as dramatic as those of the student just described, but all students must go through the process of reassessing their values and beliefs as they adopt new modes of thinking. Personal barriers to critical thinking may seem most natural and evident in disciplines like religion, philosophy, art, or literature, but even in the sciences and mathematics there is a personal element to critical thinking. As long as teachers assume that they can foster critical thinking merely by presenting an appropriate analytical perspective for their discipline, they will be unable to cope with students whose difficulties lie in this personal and subjective realm.

Integrating Personal Elements in Critical Thinking

Unfortunately, understanding potential personal barriers to critical thinking and overcoming those barriers are two very different things. How can teachers move students from, say, a position of dualism to one of multiplicity? What teaching strategies and classroom atmosphere will facilitate students' letting go of, or reframing, the values and commitments that impede their thinking abilities?

One of the least talked about, yet most important, aspects of teaching critical thinking is the provision of an atmosphere of trust and support wherein students can let go of some of the personal moorings that impose limitations on the ways they think. Too much has been made of the teacher as authority figure and taskmaster and not enough of the teacher as coach, cheerleader, and source of support. Yet any teacher who has worked with students who have learning disabilities, with adults returning to college after years of absence, or even with ordinary college students who are having difficulty knows that support and encouragement are every bit as important as providing discipline content or frameworks for analysis. I expect this is why teachers' own personalities often play such a key role in helping students adopt new modes of thinking. A teacher's enthusiasm, interest, and genuine concern help create a challenging yet safe atmosphere in which students feel confident enough to let go of old ways of thinking and try out new ones.

Support can be provided in a number of ways, big and small. Validating students' contributions to class discussion or writing encouraging comments on their written assignments are ways of letting them know that their efforts are taken seriously. Making encouraging nods, showing patience as students struggle to express themselves, drawing parallels between students' own experiences and the subject being taught help to show confidence in students' ability to think critically. Students need classroom environments where they know their own experiences and convictions will be respected. Only in such an environment will teachers be in a position to provide both the challenges and the support necessary to encourage new modes of critical thinking.

The personal elements involved in teaching, and learning all tie together. The insights of Jean Piaget, Michael Polanyi, and William Perry, though from different disciplines, provide a congruent and helpful frame of reference for considering the difficulties teachers often encounter in teaching their students to think critically. Before arriving at college, most students have already formulated personal perspectives on the world. They are not likely to easily abandon those interpretations, and teachers who assume that all that needs to be done is to expose students to new interpretations are seriously underestimating the task at hand. By appreciating the very personal nature of critical thinking, teachers are more likely to successfully challenge old perspectives, offer models for new ones, and provide adequate support for students to try out new values and points of view.

Relatedly, instructors also need the permission and courage to reveal personal and subjective elements in their teaching and thinking. When teachers model their own values, interests, and critical thinking styles, they give students concrete alternatives to react to as the students attempt to define their own values and thinking styles. Just as small children formulate their values and thought structures by observing, imitating, and challenging those of their peers and significant adults, so college students will learn by reacting to their instructors. By adopting a more personal mode of teaching and by acknowledging the personal nature of learning, teachers can provide students with the models they need in order to understand and integrate the personal elements in their own thinking.

8

Becoming Teachers of Critical Thinking: A Seminar Model

What practical resources are available to instructors who want to become better teachers of critical thinking? In raising this question, we must face the fact that few college and university teachers have any training in general teaching skills, let alone skills in teaching critical thinking. Most teachers come to the profession fresh from graduate school and total immersion in areas of specialization far removed from undergraduate teaching concerns. The specialist mentality, nurtured by most graduate schools, often isolates new teachers from their colleagues and contributes to the loneliness that seems to pervade the profession. The lack of training in general teaching skills only exacerbates this isolation, making many teachers feel ill equipped to face the challenges of teaching critical thinking and reluctant to share their misgivings and feelings of inadequacy with others. In such a context it is not surprising that college teachers seldom seek each other's assistance in improving their teaching skills. Those who eventually become good teachers do so on their own, perhaps modeling their methods and style on teachers they had in undergraduate and graduate school, and always struggling through a painfully slow and tiresome process of trial and error.

Initiating Dialogue: Limitations of Traditional Approaches

The teaching profession desperately needs some way to break through isolation and create both dialogue and practical structures that allow teachers to share with each other their collective concerns and wisdom. Every college and university has its core of dedicated and competent teachers, and most teachers care about their students' thinking abilities. But it is difficult to share much information about the teaching of critical thinking in institutions where there is little dialogue about teaching in general.

In my opinion, traditional avenues of professional development offer few opportunities to learn the craft of teaching critical thinking. Sabbatical leaves, grant-supported research, and advanced coursework seldom deal with teaching concerns and are typically carried out in isolation from others. Professional conferences have not fared much better as a means of stimulating dialogue about teaching. Historically, such conferences have reflected the worst tradition of academia—a passive format in which teachers themselves are lectured to on esoteric topics far removed from everyday teaching concerns.

Happily, things are beginning to change. More articles about teaching in general, and the teaching of critical thinking in particular, are becoming available. Several publications devoted exclusively to the teaching enterprise have appeared, with the New Directions for Teaching and Learning series (Jossey-Bass) and *College Teaching* (Heldref Publications) providing particularly fine resources for interested teachers.

On the conference circuit, increasing numbers of professional associations are showing concern for the teaching enterprise and, in many instances, formal presentation of papers is being replaced by workshop formats that foster an active interchange of ideas. In a break from the tradition of discipline-specific conferences, national conferences with an interdisciplinary focus on critical thinking are being offered. In recent years the University of Chicago, through its Continuing Education Program, has offered a series of national conferences, including "Developmental Theory, Critical Thinking, and Liberal Education," "Critical Thinking and the Formation of Values," and "Writing, Meaning, and Higher Order Reasoning," all aimed at improving the teaching of critical thinking. The Center for Critical Thinking and Moral Critique at Sonoma State University in California has also offered a series of national and international conferences on critical thinking.*

Conferences of this nature provide an excellent opportunity for developing contact with colleagues at other institutions and for stimulating dialogue about the teaching of critical thinking. But questions must be raised about the overall effectiveness of such approaches in bringing about significant changes in *teaching practice*. Changes in teaching practice are often difficult to implement, as most of us know from personal experience. It is natural to be excited by reading a book or article or attending a conference, and equally natural to tuck the newly discovered information away in some soon-to-be-forgotten file. The chasm between insight and action is difficult to bridge.

Three elements usually missing from books, journals, conferences, and workshops are needed to help teachers learn how to teach critical thinking. They are sufficient time for teachers to clarify the nature of their own approaches to critical thinking, an atmosphere of support in which colleagues encourage each other to develop new strategies for teaching critical thinking, and accountability for implementing those strategies. Most teachers will not make significant changes in their teaching practice unless all three elements are present. In the remainder of this chapter we will investigate a teaching seminar project that successfully incorporates these elements into a practical model for training faculty in the teaching of critical thinking.

Metropolitan State University Teaching Seminars

Since its establishment in 1971, Metropolitan State University (Metro U) of St. Paul, Minnesota, has functioned as a university where teaching takes precedence over research. Metro U was created as an alternative, competence-based university for

*For more information about these programs, write to the University of Chicago, Continuing Education Programs, 1307 East 60th Street, Chicago, Illinois 60637, and to Sonoma State University, Center for Critical Thinking and Moral Critique, Rohnert Park, California 94928.

adults whose educational needs were not being met by traditional institutions. David Sweet, one of the founders and the first president of the university, proclaimed, "There are all too few institutions of higher education, particularly public institutions of higher education, which are devoted exclusively to *teaching* students. This college will become such an institution. And it will seek out and retain faculty members who are prepared to share that commitment" (1971, pp. 22-23).

To carry out its commitment to competence-based education and its focus on good teaching, Metro U relies on practicing professionals—community faculty—as its primary teaching resource. A much smaller number of resident faculty serves to coordinate and supervise the work of the community faculty. The university presently supports a staff of thirty-five resident and over five hundred community faculty—a ratio of one to fifteen. Resident faculty spend most of their time developing the curriculum and helping community faculty improve their teaching skills. Initially this latter duty presented a challenge; for, as in most traditional faculties, few of Metro U's resident faculty had formal training in teaching theory or methodology. During the university's early years, resident faculty spent much time talking about teaching strategies and developing methods for sharing that information with one another and with community faculty.

Similarly, although many community faculty members had some practice in developing educational materials or leading workshops related to their professions, few had any experience with extended college teaching. Even fewer had explicitly taught their areas of expertise from a critical thinking perspective. Yet, for many reasons, Metro U could not afford the slow, often painful, initiation into teaching that most universities rely on.

In its early years, Metro U relied on a traditional workshop format as a means of improving community faculty teaching skills. Student evaluations indicated a high level of satisfaction with the quality of its teaching, but there was still evidence that many teachers were relying on traditional methods of presentation (primarily lecture) and that students were not getting sufficient opportunities to develop and apply their own thinking skills. Metro U teachers themselves also persistently complained that their students, while rich in practical experience, lacked the analytical skills expected of them. Finally, the faculty leading "teaching skill" workshops reported feeling that, despite good attendance by community faculty and generally lively discussions, the workshops were not really changing teaching practice.

In the fall of 1980, with these concerns in mind, Metro U began exploring an alternative to the teaching skill workshops—the teaching *seminar* (Meyers, 1984). One of the most important considerations in the development of the seminars was that they be long term: Participating faculty were asked to make a commitment to a series of six monthly meetings. A second important feature was a focus on practice teaching. During the six months, each faculty member was expected to teach two minilessons before the group. A third crucial element was the seminar's reliance on peer leadership. Though one faculty member agreed to serve as general coordinator-facilitator, leadership participation was expected and indeed demanded of all present. Finally, in the best tradition of adult learning, the seminars were self-paced. A general outline and agenda were presented at the first group meeting, but once they were initiated, seminars proceeded at their own pace.

The first teaching seminar was composed of eight faculty members representing different disciplines. While the initial focus of the seminar was not explicitly on the teaching of critical thinking but rather on the integration of theory and practice, it soon became clear that the two were inseparable. The stated goal of the seminar was for teachers to clarify the exact nature of what they were trying to teach their students, in terms of both theoretical components and practical applications. Each participant was asked to address the question, "What do you want students to *know* and *be able to do* at the completion of your course?" The "to do" aspect of participants' answers usually proved to be a list of critical analytical skills or the application of some analytical framework. Teachers were also asked to analyze their present methods of testing and evaluating students and to determine whether those methods actually evaluated what they were trying to teach.

The seminar met regularly one evening a month for three hours and ran from November to April. Meetings were held in faculty homes, and the informal atmosphere did much to facilitate sharing of mutual teaching concerns. The mix of disciplines helped avoid internecine debates that might have characterized a group of, say, eight literature teachers arguing strictly literary concerns. Each participant assumed that the others knew their disciplines and was thus free to learn from them without arguing differences in disciplinary perspective.

The most exciting aspect of the seminar was the opportunity it gave teachers to practice teaching in front of their peers. As part of the exercise in clarifying teaching objectives, each participant was asked to prepare a minilesson introducing his or her course to the group, as might be done on the first night of class. Faculty handed out copies of course syllabi and addressed the group as they would students. Each faculty member was allotted ten minutes to introduce his or her course and to state clearly its objectives and practical learning outcomes. After the presentation was over, group members critiqued it for clarity and raised questions about the reality of accomplishing stated goals in a normal academic quarter. The teachers often were embarrassed to discover that what had seemed clear to them individually was not always clear to the group.

As the seminar proceeded, it became clear that a major component of everyone's course involved the development of some analytical framework or disciplinary perspective. Indeed, most of the six months was spent in clarifying those frameworks and perspectives. Perhaps the most important outcomes of the seminar, however, were concrete changes in teaching practice. With the support of their peers, teachers took back to their classrooms the materials developed in the seminar (revised syllabi and student assignments) and put them into practice. They reported on the success or failure of these efforts and made changes in teaching strategies when necessary.

When time came for the seminar to disband, in April of 1981, the group decided unanimously to reconvene the following fall and to spend another six months working on their teaching concerns. During their second year together, faculty continued to work on clarifying teaching objectives. They also began videotaping one another in live teaching situations and then reviewing and critiquing the results. None of this could have happened had the group not developed a high level of trust during its first year together. At the end of the second year, the group disbanded, but individual members went on to help lead ensuing seminars.

Seminars in Critical Thinking: Teachers Teaching Teachers

During the following year, a new seminar with a specific focus on the teaching of critical thinking was initiated. The theme of critical thinking was implicit during the first year, but it became explicit as a result of my own work on critical thinking during a year's fellowship and Carol Holmberg's work on visualizing disciplinary frameworks, described in Chapter Two of this book. The critical thinking seminar was the same as the initial seminar in size, meeting time, and format. Again, group members were a disciplinary mix, though this time all participants were selected from the humanities disciplines; history, philosophy, religion, literature, art, and anthropology were represented.

One faculty member agreed to serve as group facilitator, but, as before, the seminar operated on the principle of peer leadership, with individuals sharing equal responsibility for teaching minilessons. In preparation for the first session, faculty received a mailing detailing general seminar goals and expectations, as shown in Exhibit 13. At the first meeting, a resource person introduced the idea of disciplinary frameworks as one way to think about the teaching of critical thinking. Piaget's concept of "structures of thought" was also offered as a metaphor for the development of new modes of problem solving and analysis.

After this introduction, participants were asked to share specific examples of the problems or issues they wanted students to be able to analyze. They were also asked to discuss the critical skills and analytical framework they wanted their students to learn. Through this discussion, it became clear that many different analytical frameworks were represented in the group and also that, even when pressed, most teachers had a difficult time explaining

Exhibit 13. Critical Thinking Seminar Agenda.

Format. The Teaching Seminar differs from Metro U's one-day workshops in that the same small group of faculty will be meeting together for a period of six months. The purpose of the seminar is to help us clarify individual concepts of critical thinking and improve the teaching of those concepts. The group is composed of eight resident and community faculty. Tuesday afternoons from 2 to 5 P.M. seem the best meeting time, so, unless conflicts arise, we will meet the first Tuesday of each month between October and March.

Seminar Goals

1. To clarify our teaching objectives in regard to critical thinking. What is the exact nature of the critical-analytical process we want students to learn?
2. To critique our written assignments and see if they reflect the critical thinking skills we have identified.
3. To develop a sense of collegiality about matters of teaching and use each other as teaching resources.

Responsibilities. Choose one course you teach regularly and want to work on improving. During the next six months, you will teach two ten-minute minilessons in front of the group: one explaining your framework for critical thinking and one describing a critical thinking assignment. Prepare these presentations as you would for your students. The group will first play the role of student and then critique your materials from a professional perspective. *Fear not!* Critiques are always done with care and tenderness—everyone knows his or her turn to be critiqued will come. The major assumption of the seminars is that if we cannot communicate our teaching intentions clearly to fellow teachers, we probably will not be able to communicate them to our students.

Schedule

Oct. 1	Intro. to seminars, concepts of disciplinary frameworks, mental structures, and visual models
Nov. 5	Minilessons on critical thinking models
Dec. 3	Minilessons (continued)
Jan. 7	Minilessons on written assignments
Feb. 4	Minilessons (continued)
Mar. 4	Presentation of revised materials, final evaluation

exactly what they meant by the term *critical thinking*. A common theme was "I know what critical thinking is when I see it, but I can't describe it exactly or tell you how I teach it." The first session ended with a brief presentation by Carol Holmberg, who showed how she had used visualization to clarify her own disciplinary framework for critical thinking.

In preparation for the second and third seminar meetings, each teacher was asked to prepare a one-page description of the critical thinking process or analytical framework he or she wanted students to learn. In so doing, participants were encouraged to make explicit their own personal approaches to disciplinary analysis and to provide a visualization of that process, as Holmberg had suggested. Participants were also asked to include in their one-page descriptions a concrete example of how this critical thinking process worked in practice, that is, to show the analysis of an actual issue or problem from the point of view of their disciplines. The instruction sheet for this assignment is shown in Exhibit 14.

Presentations followed the same format as in the first seminar. Again, teachers had ten minutes to present a minilesson simulating their first meeting with a class. This time, however, the focus was on explaining to students the nature of a disciplinary framework for critical analysis. After fifteen minutes of feedback and clarification, each participant was asked to use this information to develop a revised and improved description and visualization of his or her framework for critical thinking. Two full seminar meetings were required for all eight participants to teach and discuss their minilessons.

In the fourth and fifth meetings, each participant presented (via minilesson) a written assignment that required students to exercise the critical analytical skills he or she had described. Through this process the teachers discovered how ambiguous and open to misinterpretation most of their assignments were. Once again, participants were asked to incorporate the feedback from this discussion into the creation of a revised written assignment. The minilessons on written assignments also required two full seminar meetings. The instruction sheet for this second assignment is shown in Exhibit 15.

Exhibit 14. Teaching Seminar Assignment 1.

For our next meeting, prepare a ten-minute minilesson introducing your course to a new class of students. Concentrate on the critical thinking process you want students to learn. Bring with you eight copies of a syllabus or course outline. In addition to the syllabus, bring eight copies of the following materials:

1. A one-page description of your course, listing two major objectives (content and methodology) and explaining the type of critical thinking process you want students to learn. In preparing your description it might help to try to complete this sentence: "By the end of this class, I want you [student] to be able to . . . " Provide a concrete example of a problem and its solution by this process.
2. On a separate piece of paper, try to picture what this critical thinking process looks like. Think in terms of a disciplinary perspective or framework. It might help to look at the visual models we distributed at the first meeting.

The above assignment should take about two hours. Once you have completed the written and visual description, prepare your ten-minute presentation. In order to get through all the presentations in two meetings, we will have to stay close to this time limit. After your presentation, we will spend fifteen minutes on suggestions and feedback.

At the sixth and final meeting, each teacher distributed to the group a revised written and visual one-page description of his or her analytical framework for critical thinking and a revised critical thinking assignment, taking ten minutes to explain the revisions. The final hour was given over to an evaluation of the entire seminar.

Response to the critical thinking seminar was overwhelmingly positive. The mutuality of the struggle created an atmosphere of support in which all participants felt free to acknowledge doubts and difficulties related to their teaching of critical thinking. This supportive environment, coupled with adequate time to work through individual concepts of critical thinking in the context of specific disciplines and the accountability for completing seminar assignments, encouraged most participants to incorporate some of the seminar materials into actual classroom experience. Thus, the

Exhibit 15. Teaching Seminar Assignment 2.

Your assignment for the next meeting is to bring eight copies of a written assignment that you think requires students to exercise the critical thinking skills you are trying to teach them. You will have ten minutes to present this assignment to the group and to field questions from the "students." In preparation for this presentation, you may want to do your own critique of the assignment. If this results in a revision of the assignment, all the better. Consider the following questions in your critique.

1. What is the specific goal of this assignment? What kinds of knowledge and levels of understanding do you want students to demonstrate?
2. Is the assignment clearly stated and unambiguous? Are there any ways students might logically misinterpret your directions?
3. How does the goal of this assignment reflect the analytical framework of critical thinking you are trying to teach?

For practice, have some fun critiquing and *misinterpreting* the following essay questions:

- In Henry James's *The Americans,* do you agree with Newman that Mademoiselle Nioche is a "frank coquette"?
- What do you think of Reinhold Niebuhr's argument against classical Marxism?
- What is Carol Gilligan doing in Chapter 4 of *In a Different Voice*?

---

seminar succeeded in its attempt to foster concrete changes in teaching behavior. There were also at least three tangible results from the critical thinking seminar in that, by the end of the six months, each participant had a written and visual description of a disciplinary framework for critical thinking and analysis, a revised written assignment that clearly and explicitly required application of that framework, and a resource pool of seven colleagues who could be called upon for future assistance and could serve as a continuing source of dialogue about critical thinking at the university.

This teaching seminar model provides a simple yet effective means of improving the teaching of critical thinking. Because seminars rely on the resourcefulness of the participants rather than on visiting experts, seminar members are more willing to take the lead in sharing teaching concerns and devising ways to improve teaching. Six three-hour meetings spread over six months provide sufficient time to develop this enterprise. The support and accountability of regular meetings and assignments do much to foster real changes in teaching practice. Finally, through the creation of this formal structure, the seminars also serve as a catalyst for an expanding dialogue about teaching critical thinking—something most colleges and universities could profit from.

Critical Thinking Seminars at Other Universities

Metro U's critical thinking seminar is not the only successful model for teachers teaching teachers. In Chapter Three, we discussed the work of the ADAPT faculty at the University of Nebraska at Lincoln in forming groups of teachers to study Piaget and implement learning cycle models for undergraduate students. In his paper on study groups at the University of North Dakota, Henry B. Slotnik (1984) reports on the use of practice teaching and videotaping to improve instructional skills. Through a grant from the Fund for the Improvement of Postsecondary Education (FIPSE), the University of Minnesota has also experimented with faculty seminars based on a "consultant model," in which consultants observed actual teaching practice and then, through ongoing seminars, gave teachers feedback on their instruction and support for improving it. Jane Lawson attributes the success of these teaching seminars to the support they provided for teachers trying to make difficult and sometimes painful changes in teaching methodology. "To have the opportunity to talk about their successes and failures, feelings of accomplishment and frustration, to be able to exchange ideas and get help from other professors provides a support base for the professors who are faced with the challenge presented by having one's classes observed and receiving feedback on one's teaching" (p. 5). Clearly, college teachers' ability to teach each other the skills and attitudes of critical thinking is a resource worthy of consideration.

One of the main advantages of Metropolitan State University's particular critical thinking seminar model is the ease with which it can be used by other colleges and universities. Although Metro U is unique in its reliance on a community, or adjunct, faculty, there would seem to be little difficulty in adapting its model to use at more traditional universities. The following specific features of the Metro U seminar seem particularly worthy of inclusion in programs developed by other schools.

- *Voluntary participation.* One of the main reasons for the success of the seminars is their entirely voluntary nature. An effort is made to portray the seminars as a special opportunity for a limited number of participants. Interest in participation is solicited early in the academic year, through registration at an annual fall conference.
- *Support of university administrators.* Although participation is voluntary, it is important that seminars be officially sanctioned by the academic vice president. At Metro U, community faculty are each paid a stipend of $250 for their participation. Resident faculty are not paid but are given compensatory leave time and are encouraged to incorporate the seminar into their annual professional development plans, filed with the vice president.
- *Interdisciplinary mix of participants.* A mix of disciplines avoids intradisciplinary debates and adds the richness of different perspectives to the exploration of critical thinking concepts. For example, a professor of management theory offered a framework for critical thinking that a philosophy teacher used to clarify his own critical thinking perspective.
- *Good facilitation.* The success of the seminars rises or falls on the skill of the facilitator. Therefore, although peer leadership often emerges, it is crucial that one faculty member be competent as a general facilitator, helping the group stick to its agenda and making sure that individual presentations stay within the given time limit. A good facilitator will also encourage reticent members to participate and gently "sit on" overly verbal members. Since the facilitator is also a participant, this can be a tricky role.

- *Structured agenda and specific monthly assignments.* Once instructors start talking openly about their teaching concerns, there is a tendency for discussion to wander from the original task. Adherence to an agreed-upon agenda helps avoid a "bull session" atmosphere that, while very convivial, is unproductive of concrete outcomes. A set of structured assignments and a schedule for presentation of minilessons help keep the participants on schedule.

9

Why Critical Thinking Should Be a Part of Every Course

Today both teachers and students have at their hands an overwhelming abundance of information. Teachers sometimes despair of knowing how all these new developments in their disciplines can be sorted through to determine what students need to know. Students feel the onslaught of the information age even more acutely than their teachers and are less capable of coping with its demands and of making sense of the complex world it presents. College teachers can help their students cope with this complexity by suggesting analytical frameworks and perspectives for sorting things out and thinking critically about them.

Critical thinking abilities do not develop unaided during a course of study, nor will they arise solely from students' listening to lectures, reading texts, and taking exams. Teachers must know explicitly what they mean by *critical thinking* in the context of their disciplines and must provide opportunities for students to practice critical thinking skills and attitudes. Attempting to visualize analytical frameworks, sharing their own methods of problem solving with students, talking with colleagues, engaging in faculty seminars—by these means or any others, teachers in all disciplines need to assume responsibility for teaching the skills and attitudes of critical inquiry.

In addition to teaching explicit skills and analytical frameworks, teachers must nurture attitudinal aspects of critical thinking—students' innate sources of interest, wonder, and inquisitiveness. Whitehead's ([1929] 1967, p. 36) comment on student interest as the *sine qua non* of all learning has a ring of truth about it that few can dispute. Significant learning usually takes place only when learners are motivated by some sense of wonder, mystery, and personal interest. All of us who teach must be prepared to create that interest.

It is a good idea for teachers occasionally to step back from immersion in their disciplines and try to see their subject matter through the eyes of an outsider. This means taking seriously student misgivings and misperceptions. Why in heaven's name would anyone want to understand the meaning of Hamlet's soliloquy, the nature of photosynthesis, Kant's categorical imperative, the tribal rites of the Trobriand Islanders? If we do not approach our own disciplines with at least some of the misgivings that students do, we will never appreciate the crucial role we need to play in stimulating student interest and generating motivation for learning to think critically.

Creating classroom environments that encourage discussion, questioning, probing, and pondering will go a long way toward fostering critical thinking. Such environments can be developed partly by structuring classroom time to include more discussion and by designing clear, effective written assignments. The incorporation of reading materials that foster student interest is also important. The traditional college textbook is often boring stuff. We need more academic writers like Lewis Thomas and Stephen Jay Gould, whose work is a testimony that scientific accuracy need not be boring or obfuscating. By carefully selecting texts and assigned readings on the basis of clarity and contagion, we can help students overcome negative attitudes toward subject matter and introduce them to the pleasurable activity that learning can and should be.

Assuming such an interest-oriented approach to teaching can be very threatening, as long as teaching is viewed as somehow having to do with the "professing" of certain disciplinary "truths." Yet each of us knows that "truth" is constantly being redefined in our respective disciplines. Perhaps it is time to begin acknowledging that the aim of teaching is not so much the provision of truth to the uninitiated as it is the teaching of various perspectives on different kinds of "truths."

This book departs from traditional approaches to critical thinking primarily by emphasizing that critical thinking is best taught through a variety of disciplinary perspectives that incorporate subjective elements of knowledge. Too much discussion of critical thinking focuses either on the discipline of logic or on general skills in problem solving. As long as critical thinking is conceived of exclusively as a form of logic or some watered-down version of the scientific method, the focus will remain purely instrumental, objective, and impersonal. Critical thinking needs to be freed from such a narrow frame of reference and expanded to include a variety of more openly subjective and personal perspectives.

The logical-objective methodology that dominates the sciences is only one of many critical thinking perspectives that can help us make sense of the world and order our experiences. Ironically, while leading scientific theoreticians such as Michael Polanyi and respected writers such as Lewis Thomas and Carl Sagan have begun to acknowledge that the claims of science to objectifiably verifiable truth have been overstated, the bulk of college students and lay individuals continue to look to science as a source of authority and certainty. Perhaps our society's continued faith in science and students' search for certainty are only reflections of a culture dominated by dualistic thinking. Students need to appreciate both the contributions and the relativity of the scientific perspective, and they need to realize that each academic discipline offers its own unique window on reality.

Students also need to appreciate the important role that personal values, interests, and passions play in creating different disciplinary perspectives. There is much to be gained by allowing the teaching of critical thinking to include personal and subjective elements. Teaching critical thinking in a detached, logical, "objective" perspective makes learning a serious and often boring endeavor. American education needs an infusion of wonder, mystery, passion, and caring to bring it to life. While the best critical thinking in any discipline will always entail the creation of well-formed judgments and healthy doses of skepticism and objectivity, the best critical thinkers also care passionately about what they study.

Most teachers do care passionately about their disciplines. They did not slip into the study of their respective disciplines merely through some disinterested pursuit of knowledge for knowledge's sake. All teachers have a personal concern about that which they study, and the best teaching communicates that caring to others. If we can teach our students to care about and respect a multiplicity of perspectives, we will have gone a long way toward making them truly educated persons. We will also have given them something far more important than a variety of detached analytical schemas. By teaching them to care about what they study, we may also encourage them to preserve what they study, so it can be passed on to others.

What we are talking about here involves a question of values and the overall aims of education. Commenting on Americans' faith in education, Malcolm Knowles observes, "The faith has been if we simply pour enough knowledge into people: (1) they will turn out to be good people, and (2) they will know how to make use of their knowledge" (1980, p. 18). Though most of us have been disabused of the equation of knowledge and virtue, it has taken Watergate, Vietnam, and the threat of nuclear weapons in space to drive that message home. The men who masterminded Watergate were educated at the best colleges and universities in the country. They were some of the "brightest," though clearly not the "best," thinkers in political power. Vietnam became a testing ground for incredibly destructive military technology conceived by brilliant minds in our Defense Department and produced by the genius of men and women in American industry. These people possessed great technical knowledge but apparently lacked the ability to step back and evaluate the uses to which they were asked to put it.

We are all aware of the limitations of the logical-objective scientific perspective in dealing with matters of the heart and answering questions that have to do with our overall quality of life. While we may not be able to teach our students wisdom and virtue, we can at least—by openly incorporating appropriate subjective elements of wonder, beauty, and passion in our courses—expose them to the caring side of knowledge. Perhaps by teaching students to appreciate the richness and diversity that our disciplines have to offer, we can also encourage them to preserve that richness and diversity. If a student of biology truly appreciates the wonder and complexity of a freshwater pond, that student will probably be concerned with preventing water pollution. If we teach our students to care, or at least show them that we care, our teaching of critical thinking may foster a future technology more concerned with healing than with destruction. Then students may learn that the wonders of life on our frail planet are not only puzzles that engage our problem-solving abilities but also mysteries worthy of preserving simply for the beauty and joy they offer.

References

Ashton, P. T. "Cross Cultural Piagetian Research: An Experimental Perspective." In *Stage Theories of Cognitive and Moral Development.* Reprint no. 13. Cambridge, Mass.: Harvard Educational Review, 1978.

Black, M. *Critical Thinking.* Englewood Cliffs, N.J.: Prentice-Hall, 1952.

Bransford, J. *Human Cognition.* Belmont, Calif.: Wadsworth, 1979.

Carmichael, J. W. "Improving Problem-Solving Skills: Minority Students in Health Professions." In K. V. Lauridsen and C. Meyers (eds.), *Summer Programs for Underprepared Freshmen.* New Directions for College Learning Assistance, no. 10. San Francisco: Jossey-Bass, 1982.

Christensen, C. R. *Teaching by the Case Method.* (Rev. ed.) Boston: Division of Research, Harvard Business School, forthcoming (Fall 1986).

Corner, M. *Adaptable Writing Assignments: Summaries.* Mankato, Minn.: Valley Writing Project, Mankato State University, 1983.

Dewey, J. *How We Think.* Lexington, Mass.: Heath, 1982. (Originally published 1910.)

Eakins, B., and Eakins, R. G. *Sex Differences in Human Communication.* Boston: Houghton Mifflin, 1978.

Eble, K. E. *The Aims of College Teaching.* San Francisco: Jossey-Bass, 1983.

Elkind, D. "Piagetian and Psychometric Conceptions of Intelligence." In *Stage Theories of Cognitive and Moral Development:*

Criticisms and Applications. Reprint no. 13. Cambridge, Mass.: Harvard Educational Review, 1978.

Emig, J. "Writing as a Mode of Learning." *College Composition and Communication,* 1977, *28,* 122-128.

Ennis, R. "A Concept of Critical Thinking." *Harvard Educational Review,* 1962, *32,* 81-111.

Fields, C. M. "Medical Schools Urged to Stress Critical Thinking." *Chronicle of Higher Education,* 1984, *29* (5), 1, 15.

Fuller, R. G. *Multidisciplinary Piagetian-Based Programs for College Freshmen.* Lincoln: University of Nebraska at Lincoln Press, 1977.

Gilligan, C. *In a Different Voice.* Cambridge, Mass.: Harvard University Press, 1982.

Gould, S. J. "A Biological Homage to Mickey Mouse." In *The Panda's Thumb.* New York: Norton, 1980.

Gremore, R. "Designing Writing Assignments for Your Class." Unpublished paper, Prairie Writing Project, Metropolitan State University, St. Paul, Minn., 1983.

Hill, W. F. *Learning Through Discussion.* Beverly Hills, Calif.: Sage, 1969.

Holmberg, C. "Using Visual Paradigms in Classroom Teaching." Unpublished report, State Universities of Minnesota, Sept. 1982.

Holt, J. *How Children Fail.* (Rev. ed.) New York: Dell, 1982.

Hudgins, B. *Learning and Thinking.* Itasca, Ill.: Peacock, 1978.

Hunt, M. "Do You Know How You Think?" *Minneapolis Star and Tribune,* May 12, 1982a, p. 13A.

Hunt, M. *The Universe Within: A New Science Explores the Human Mind.* New York: Simon & Schuster, 1982b.

Jones, R. *Physics as Metaphor.* Minneapolis: University of Minnesota Press, 1983.

Karplus, R., and others. *Science Teaching and the Development of Reasoning.* Berkeley, Calif.: Lawrence Hall of Science, University of California, 1978.

Kinney, J. A. "Why Bother? The Importance of Critical Thinking." In R. E. Young (ed.), *Fostering Critical Thinking.* New Directions for Teaching and Learning, no. 3. San Francisco: Jossey-Bass, 1980.

Knowles, M. *The Modern Practice of Adult Education.* (Rev. ed.) Chicago: Follett, 1980.

Kohlberg, L. "Stage and Sequence: The Cognitive-Developmental Approach to Socialization." In D. A. Goslin (ed.), *Handbook of Socialization Theory and Research.* Skokie, Ill.: Rand McNally, 1969.

Kolodiy, G. "The Cognitive Development of High School and College Science Students." *Journal of College Science Teaching,* 1975, *5* (1), 20-22.

Lawson, A., and Renner, J. "Piagetian Theory and Biology Teaching." *The American Biology Teacher,* 1975, *37* (6), 336-343.

Lawson, J. "The Consultation Model of Teaching Improvement." Unpublished manuscript, University of Minnesota, n.d.

Lipman, M. "Philosophy for Children." *Metaphilosophy,* 1976, *7* (1), 17-40.

Loacker, G. "Revitalizing the Academic Disciplines by Clarifying Objectives." In G. Loacker and E. G. Palola (eds.), *Clarifying Learning Outcomes in the Liberal Arts.* New Directions for Experiential Learning, no. 12. San Francisco: Jossey-Bass, 1981.

Loacker, G., and others. *Analysis and Communication at Alverno: An Approach to Critical Thinking.* Milwaukee: Alverno Productions, 1984.

McFague, S. *Speaking in Parables.* Philadelphia: Fortress Press, 1975.

McKeachie, W. J. *Teaching Tips: A Guidebook for the Beginning Teacher.* (6th ed.) Lexington, Mass.: Heath, 1969.

McKeon, R. *Aristotle's Rhetoric: An Introduction to Aristotle.* (2nd ed.) Chicago: University of Chicago Press, 1974.

McPeck, J. *Critical Thinking and Education.* New York: St. Martin's Press, 1981.

McPeck, J. "Stalking Beasts, but Swatting Flies: The Teaching of Critical Thinking." *Canadian Journal of Education,* 1984, *9* (1), 28-44.

Meyers, C. "Quality Teaching and Adjunct Faculty: Expectations, Structures, and Dialogue." In *Proceedings of Sixth Annual Conference on Quality in Off-Campus Credit Programs:*

Challenges, Choices, and Concerns. Issues in Higher Education. Manhattan: Kansas State University, 1984.

Moore, W. E., McCann, H., and McCann, J. *Creative and Critical Thinking.* Boston: Houghton Mifflin, 1985.

Norman, D. "What Goes On in the Mind of the Learner." In W. J. McKeachie (ed.), *Learning, Cognition, and College Teaching.* New Directions for Teaching and Learning, no. 2. San Francisco: Jossey-Bass, 1980.

Nouwen, H. *Reaching Out.* New York: Doubleday, 1966.

Perry, W. *Forms of Intellectual and Ethical Development in the College Years: A Scheme.* New York: Holt, Rinehart & Winston, 1970.

Perry, W. "Cognitive and Ethical Growth: The Making of Meaning." In A. W. Chickering (ed.), *The Modern American College: Responding to the New Realities of Diverse Students and a Changing Society.* San Francisco: Jossey-Bass, 1981.

Piaget, J. "Cognitive Development in Children: Development and Learning." *Journal of Research in Science Teaching,* 1964, *2,* 176–186.

Piaget, J. *Psychology of Intelligence.* Totowa, N.J.: Littlefield Adams, 1976. (Originally published 1947.)

Polanyi, M. *Personal Knowledge: Towards a Post-Critical Philosophy.* Chicago: University of Chicago Press, 1962.

Sanders, N. *Classroom Questions: What Kinds?* New York: Harper & Row, 1966.

Slotnik, H. "The Study Group: Faculty Helping Themselves to Improve Their Instructional Abilities." Unpublished paper, University of North Dakota, Grand Forks, 1984.

Smith, D. G. "College Classroom Interactions and Critical Thinking." *Journal of Educational Psychology,* 1977, *69* (2), 180–190.

Sweeney, L. "Carl Sagan: Reviving Our Sense of Wonder." *Christian Science Monitor,* March 14, 1982, pp. B7-B10.

Sweet, D. "Prospectus II." Unpublished report, Metropolitan State University, St. Paul, Minn., 1971.

Thomas, L. "The Art of Teaching Science." *New York Times Magazine,* March 14, 1982, pp. 89–93.

Tomlinson-Keasey, C. "Formal Operations in Females Aged 11 to 54 Years of Age." *Developmental Psychology,* 1972, *6,* 364.

Whimbey, A., and Lochhead, J. *Problem Solving and Communication: A Short Course in Analytic Reasoning.* Philadelphia, Penn.: Franklin Institute Press, 1979.

Whimbey, A., and others. "Teaching Critical Reading and Analytical Reasoning in Project SOAR." *Journal of Reading,* Oct. 1980, pp. 5-10.

Whitehead, A. N. *The Aims of Education.* New York: Free Press, 1967. (Originally published 1929.)

Yinger, R. J. "Can We Really Teach Them to Think?" In R. E. Young (ed.), *Fostering Critical Thinking.* New Directions for Teaching and Learning, no. 3. San Francisco: Jossey-Bass, 1980.

Index

P

Q

R

S

T

V

W

X

Y